TAKING A STAND AGAINST
ENVIRONMENTAL POLLUTION

TAKING A STAND
AGAINST
ENVIRONMENTAL
POLLUTION

BY DAVID E. NEWTON

Franklin Watts 1990
New York London Toronto Sydney

Library of Congress Cataloging-in-Publication Data
Newton, David E.
Taking a stand against environmental pollution / David E. Newton.
p. cm.
Includes bibliographical references.
Summary: Examines current environmental issues and suggests ways
to become involved in solving problems with pollution.
ISBN 0-531-10923-2
1. Environmental protection—United States—Citizen participation—
Juvenile literature.   2. Pollution—United States—Juvenile
literature.   [1. Environmental protection.   2. Pollution.]
I. Title.
TD171.N59 1990
363.7′052—dc20   89-70562   CIP   AC

Dedicated to Doris and Jim Durant

My "other" parents,
outdoor buddies, and good friends

ACKNOWLEDGMENTS

This book contains the thoughts, ideas, and suggestions of many people active in the environmental movement. Chapters Five, Six, and Seven could never have been written without the help of those activists. The individuals listed below deserve a share of the credit for whatever value the book has for you. They bear no responsibility at all for any errors you find in these or any other chapters.

Dennis Bader, Training Student Organizers
    Program, Council on the Environment
    of New York City
Helen Barrington, Ocean Protection Coalition,
    Point Arena, California
Neva Beach, educational consultant,
    Mendocino, California
Bill Buck, former student, Santa Maria (California)
    Righetti High School
Chuck Clark, McGinnis Middle School,
    Buena Vista, Colorado

Sherena Flowers, Environmental Federation
    of California, San Francisco
Andrea Makovkin, former student,
    Mendocino (California) High School
Patricia Mayall, San Francisco
    State University Recycling Center
Michelle Miller, environmental activist,
    San Francisco
Jack Padalino, Pocono Environmental Education
    Center, Dingmans Ferry, Pennsylvania
Joan Patton, Oceanic Society, San Francisco
Charles Schwartz, community health–
    environmental consultant, Bronx, New York
William B. Stapp, School of Natural Resources,
    University of Michigan, Ann Arbor
Bonnie Tibbetts, Woodland Elementary School,
    Waite, Maine
Michael Zamm, Training Student Organizers
    Program,
Council on the Environment of New York City

CONTENTS

TAKING A STAND AGAINST
ENVIRONMENTAL POLLUTION

ONE

GETTING INVOLVED IN ENVIRONMENTAL ISSUES

When beavers build a dam, they change the natural world around them. They create a lake, where once a stream flowed. They cut down trees, allowing sunlight to penetrate where it had not gone before. They bring plant materials into their pond, changing the composition of its waters. As a result of these changes, plants and animals that were once absent from the area can now live in and around the beaver pond.

Beavers have no plans to change the living and non-living world around them—their environment—when they build a dam. Those changes come about simply as a consequence of the beavers' maintaining their own life-style.

Beavers are not unique in this respect. Every living organism, from the simplest to the most complex, affects its environment and is, in turn, affected by it. Tiny lichens that look like no more than stains on rocks are responsible for the first stage in the creation of soil from bedrock. As the lichens carry out their life processes, they secrete acids that break apart and dissolve the rock. Over long periods of time, the lichens change cold, hard, lifeless rock into soil, an environment where more complex plants can grow.

HUMANS AND THE ENVIRONMENT

No organism changes its natural environment so dramatically and with such a sense of purpose as do humans. At one time the environmental changes caused by humans were as accidental as those of beavers and lichens. But those days are very long past. For thousands of years, humans have cut down forests, changed the course of rivers, dug into mountains, created new plants and animals, erected great cities—all with the purpose of getting food, shelter, clothing, and other components of an increasingly complex life-style.

The changes that humans have made in their environment are far more extensive and far more harmful than those caused by any other organism. For example, human activities commonly bring about the extinction of other organisms, something that occurs rarely as the result of activities by other plants and animals. The Council on Environmental Quality has estimated, for example, that in the mid-1980s three species of plants and animals were dying out every day on earth. Also, one species of bird or mammal died out every year.[1] In comparison, the rate of extinction during the era when dinosaurs were dying out was one species every thousand years. The main cause of the extinctions taking place during modern times is human activity.

BECOMING AN ENVIRONMENTAL ACTIVIST

Many people are concerned about the damage that we do to our environment. Some choose to make environmentalism their career. They become ecologists, or environmental scientists, studying how the elements of nature interact with each other and how human activities affect the environment. Or they become environmental educators, teaching others about nature and the place of humans in it. Or they become environmental activists, working within the political system to bring about favorable legislation on environmental issues. You may want to consider a career in one of these fields.

But for many people, working on environmental issues is a part-time job. It's a volunteer activity in which they take part after school, after work, on weekends, or during vacations. It's an extra commitment people make to show they care about the environment.

What often happens is that a person becomes aware of an environmental issue in her or his own life and decides to start working on that issue. Bill Buck of Santa Maria, California, is one such person.

STARTING FROM GROUND UP

In many ways, Bill Buck is probably not much different from teenagers around the United States and Canada. But in some respects his life has been dramatically different from the lives of most other teenagers, and could serve as an exciting challenge to teenagers everywhere.

Environmental issues appeared somewhat abruptly in Bill's life one warm day in 1987 when Bill and many of his fellow students at Santa Maria (California) Righetti High School began to notice strange, offensive odors in the air. Some, including Bill, complained of headaches. When Bill asked around about the possible source of the foul odors, he was told that a toxic-waste dump 10 miles (16 km) from the school was probably responsible.

Bill reacted to this news differently than many of the rest of us would have. He could have said, "Oh well, that's the price of progress. Toxic chemicals have to be dumped *somewhere*. I'll just put up with this inconvenience, at least for now." But that was not Bill's response. Instead, he decided that he wanted to find out more about the toxic-waste dump, what its possible health effects might be, and what could be done about it to protect the public. The simplest approach might have been for Bill to call the Santa Maria Environmental Committee and ask it the questions he had—except that Santa Maria didn't have an environmental committee.

So, Bill took the next most likely step. He called a representative of the toxic-waste site with his questions and had them all answered in a long interview at the site. Not entirely satisfied, he went to three other people in town who were concerned and knew something about the toxic-waste dump. Some of the information he received differed from what he had been told by the representative. By the end of the interviews, Bill had decided that toxic wastes were an issue he wanted to do something about.

His first step was to write an editorial in the school newspaper, of which he was editor. That editorial stirred interest among other Righetti stu-

*Students at Righetti High School in
Santa Maria, California, protesting a proposed
toxic-waste dump near their community*

dents. Soon Bill set about organizing a student group to study and act on toxic wastes and, before long, other environmental issues in the Santa Maria area.

Probably the highlight of Bill's young career in environmentalism was the Environmental Awareness Day that he planned and carried out, an event for which Bill received one of President Reagan's Environmental Youth Awards in 1987. The all-day program consisted of speeches, video tapes, and displays on environmental topics, interspersed with live band music, songs, and other entertainment. The serious/fun contrast in the day's program reflected Bill's philosophy that in dealing with environmental issues one needs to "have a good time while learning."

Bill is also an accomplished artist and has been active in peace and antinuclear activities. In the short seventeen years of his life, Bill Buck has already shown what a difference a single teenager can make in his or her community.

Of course, the issue that interests you may not be just next door, as in Bill's case. A lot of us worry about the survival of pandas, about damage in the tropical rain forests of Brazil, and about destruction of the ozone layer in our stratosphere. Organizations working on global issues such as these exist and provide another way in which you can become active on environmental issues.

Environmental organizations are good places for teenagers to become active. Most environmental organizations are very democratic. Young and old, male and female, professionals and amateurs, and members of all racial and ethnic groups are welcome. These organizations allow teenagers to

*Bill Buck receiving a Presidential
Environmental Youth Award for his
work in organizing an Environmetal
Awareness Day at his school*

work on issues that are important to society now and that will be crucial to the future of the world and to their own futures.

WHY WORK ON ENVIRONMENTAL ISSUES?

People decide to work on environmental issues for one or more of at least three reasons: (1) for the good of nature; (2) for the good of society; and (3) for their own good.

For the Good of Nature

Most environmentalists believe that the earth is a harmonious whole in which every part is connected with every other part and every part is important. According to this philosophy, a redwood tree, a bald eagle, and a monarch butterfly all have as much right to exist as do you and I. It makes no difference what contribution, if any, an organism can make to human life, or what its economic value might be. That organism has its own right to exist on earth. Thus, when human activities threaten any part of nature, those activities need to be studied and, perhaps, brought under control.

For the Good of Society

Environmentalists do not necessarily argue that humans should not use the world around us *at all*. We

A poster for Environmental Awareness Day at Righetti High School

A scene along the Snake River in Wyoming. Environmentalists consider nature an end in itself, not simply an object of human exploitation.

need trees from which to build houses, coal with which to run factories, plants from which to get food, and so on. In fact, one goal of many environmental organizations is to make sure that valuable natural resources will be used in such a way that they will still be here in future generations.

"The good of society" means more than material benefits, however. The natural world provides many opportunities for humans to relax, learn more about themselves, about nature, and about what lies beyond nature. Whatever the phrase "the wonders of nature" means to you—hunting, fishing, hiking, camping, or simply looking at the beauty and grandeur of the natural world—environmentalists believe that those wonders should be protected for future generations.

For Your Own Good

For many people self-interest is a motive for becoming involved in environmental issues. Working on an environmental problem may help people solve a problem in their own lives, such as reducing the noise level in their own neighborhood. Or they may learn useful skills, such as how to work with others, how to organize and lead a group, or how to get things done in government. Or they may open doors to future careers, such as working professionally within the environmental movement. Or they may achieve self-satisfaction in knowing that they have spent time working on a worthwhile task that needs to be done.

Volunteer work is a noble way to use part of your leisure time. A volunteer who works on environmental issues helps protect nature in activities that bring a sense of pride and satisfaction.

In this book, you'll read about other young people who have taken a stand for our environment. You'll also learn how you can become involved in your school or community in the fight for a cleaner environment. But first let's look at how Americans responded to environmental concerns in the past.

TWO

ENVIRONMENTAL ISSUES
IN AMERICAN HISTORY

"GO FORTH AND
CONQUER THE EARTH"

Any talk of "environmental problems" among the early settlers of America at Plymouth or Jamestown would probably have seemed absurd. As a practical matter, the small number of colonists were confronted with a seemingly unlimited amount of land, with more soil, trees, minerals, wildlife, and water resources than they could ever hope to use. The notion that the pioneers might somehow represent a threat to nature would have been quite amusing to most of them.

But the overwhelming abundance of natural resources the early settlers of the United States found was not the only influence on their attitudes toward the environment. Those attitudes were also colored and shaped by the particular religious and political philosophies the colonists brought with them to the New World.

Writers such as Lynn White have described how subtly, but deeply, religious viewpoints can affect a nation's attitudes toward its natural resources.[2] He points out that Christians believe that God has given humans dominion over the earth. The Bible has, in fact, directed humans to "Be fruitful and multiply, and fill the earth and subdue it; and have dominion over the fish of the sea and over the birds of the air and over every living thing that moves upon the earth."[3]

The force of that tradition, White believes, is that many people view natural resources as something put here on earth to satisfy human needs and desires. Trees, ores, and wildlife are, in this context, "consumables" to be harvested for the use of humans. As White says, "Despite Darwin, we are *not*, in our hearts, part of the natural process. We are superior to nature, contemptuous of it, willing to use it for our slightest whim."[4]

These attitudes have continued to influence how Americans think about and act toward the environment. If a person believes the world is coming to an end in ten or twenty years, what is the point of saving resources for future generations?

This philosophy is even more important if and when it becomes part of government policy. For example, President Ronald Reagan's appointment of James Watt as his first secretary of the interior raised a storm of protest. Environmentalists feared that Watt's fundamentalist religious beliefs would influence his environmental policies. They thought that he would push for the development of natural resources rather than protecting and preserving the environment.[5]

Watt left his job at the Interior Department in 1983. The environmental philosophies for which he was criticized, however, have not disappeared. In fact, "go forth and conquer" beliefs about the environment are likely to be a factor in debates about the use of our natural resources for many years into the future.

THE AMERICAN STOREHOUSE

The political philosophy in the Colonies also influenced settlers' attitudes about their environment. Although religious freedom was an important impetus in bringing people to the United States, commercial factors were also vitally important in the Colonies' early development. Great Britain saw the Colonies as a major source of raw materials which could be shipped to the mother country, processed, and then sold back to the colonists at handsome profits. The dominant economic theme during the early years of the American nation was utilization of natural resources. Tobacco, rice, indigo, furs, timber, and fish were harvested for shipment to England.

After independence, the new United States government continued to encourage and promote the identification, extraction, and processing of our "boundless" natural resources. Federal and state governments felt that a strong, growing economy was in the best interests of the nation. They passed legislation that allowed and even encouraged private corporations to take possession of or make use of timber, land, minerals, water, and other natural resources belonging to the national and state governments. The basic principles of capitalism, the economic system of which the United States was to become the world's greatest example, by their very nature dictated a policy of aggressive and intensive resource utilization.

This review of early colonial attitudes toward the environment is not just a piece of historical trivia, of interest to scholars but irrelevant to environmental issues today. Those attitudes contributed to the development of an American environmental philosophy that continues to the present time. In most cases, the issues over which people debate today such as drilling for oil off the California coast, cutting of timber in national parks, strip-mining on federal lands, and building oil pipelines across Alaska reflect the desire of many corporations, individuals and governments to "go forth and conquer" nature, to use its abundance for our own material benefits. The progress of American environmental history over the three centuries that followed the colonial era cannot be appreciated without an understanding of that philosophy and of the opposition that has gradually developed to it.

USING THE ENVIRONMENT

As one might guess, therefore, American policies toward the environment have often been characterized by a take-and-don't-worry-about-the-consequences attitude. The timber industry is a good example of that attitude. Wood was a critical raw material for the early settlers. It was used in the building of homes, fences, and furniture; it was burned as fuel; and it was converted to charcoal and potash. The felling of trees was also necessary in the clearing of land for agriculture.

As mining, transportation, and industry developed in the young nation, the need for wood as fuel expanded. By 1775, for example, the United States was the third largest producer of iron in the world. Each of the blast furnaces used to make iron required 5 to 6 thousand cords of wood each year, which in turn required 250 acres (100 hectares) of forest. A century later, railroads were using 3 million cords of wood annually to run their engines, and another 4 million cords were required to power steamboats on the Ohio and Mississippi rivers.[6]

Yet, virtually no thought was given to the long-term effects of this massive cutting of timber. Whenever a particular area was stripped of its forests, loggers packed their equipment and moved on. There seemed to be no end to the nation's forests, so why worry about planting new trees or conserving existing supplies?

One writer has described this practice as it survived even at the end of the nineteenth century:

> *In their wake the boys left camps and sawmills where they stood. They deserted entire villages, not even bothering to pull down the blinds or take down the stovepipes. Officials of formerly well-timbered and well-taxed counties were aghast to find nothing left to eat in the public trough. Most of all, the loggers left stumps in their wake. And why not? That had been their job—to make stumps out of forests so that John Farmer, as lumberjacks somewhat disdainfully termed husbandmen, could get on with his work. No one had objected to stumps; both state and federal governments had done everything they could to get the timber cut as quickly as possible.[7]*

*The bare foreground in this photo
shows the results of unrestricted
logging. The trees still standing
in the background have
been saved by controlled logging.*

The treatment of land resources was not much different. Early farmers planted and harvested crops as long as soil could maintain its fertility. They knew or cared little about fertilizing or rotating crops, or about any other technique that would have extended the fertility of their lands. When they could no longer produce a crop, they simply moved on, cleared more forests, and started over again on new land.

Tobacco farming, a mainstay of Southern agriculture, was especially notorious in this respect. Since tobacco plants quickly use up nitrogen and potassium in the soil, a piece of land can be used for this crop for no more than about four years. After that time, most tobacco farmers simply started farming on a new piece of land.[8] Similarly, when farmers in New England depleted their land, they simply abandoned the land, moved west, and began wheat and corn production in the Midwest.[9]

Government was an eager partner in this utilization of natural resources. In action after action, the U.S. Congress gave away land, timber, minerals, and other natural resources for development by private corporations. The Swamp Act of 1850, for example, gave away 63,000,000 acres (about 25,500,000 hectares) of federal land, mostly to timber companies. Only a fraction of the land was actually swampy, and this resulted in an enormous economic windfall for timber companies.[10]

Similarly, the Preemption Act of 1841 allowed a settler and his family to buy homestead land of up to 480 acres (about 195 hectares) for 50 cents an acre. Lumber companies hired gangs of men to claim their land and hand it over to the companies. A similar practice was followed by cattle barons,

*Tobacco farming can rapidly deplete soil
of its fertility. Many early settlers
knew or cared little about fertilizing
or rotating crops. They simply moved west.*

who hired cowboys to claim homesteading lands under the Desert Land Act of 1877 and then use the lands for grazing their cattle.[11]

THE FIRST CONSERVATIONISTS

Concern for conservation of natural resources in the United States was virtually nonexistent well into the nineteenth century. Occasionally, however, someone would speak out for conservationist practices. For example, William Penn, founder of the Pennsylvania colony, had required that for every 5 acres (2 hectares) of forest cleared, 1 acre (0.4 hectare) must be left standing.[12]

When calls for conservation did begin to appear, they came from two directions. The first consisted of European scientists who had visited or emigrated to the United States and American scientists who had visited or studied in Europe or had corresponded with European scientists. They included the great Swiss naturalist Louis Agassiz and Benjamin Silliman, founder of the *American Journal of Science*. Familiar with European philosophies and practices of conservation, these scientists were often appalled at the hit-and-run approach that Americans followed in their use of natural resources. They were eager to show American farmers, ranchers, lumbermen, miners, and other utilizers of resources how to conserve those resources, that is, how to use them wisely so they would last as long as possible.

The second conservationist theme also had roots in Europe, in the works of the Romantic writers. American interpreters of this theme included

William Cullen Bryant, Ralph Waldo Emerson, and Henry David Thoreau. These writers ascribed to nature mystical, spiritual, and religious qualities. To them, nature was a pathway through which humans could reach God. In his first essay, "Nature," published in 1836, Emerson wrote that "Behind nature, throughout nature, spirit is present." Thoreau's two years at Walden Pond in 1845–46 convinced him that the fundamental truths of life are to be found in nature.

The message of these writers was quite different from that of the scientific conservationists. Their aim was not to *conserve* resources so that they could be used long into the future, but to *preserve* them, to remove them from "productive" use and set them aside in their natural state forever. For half a century, conservationists and preservationists worked side by side against the out-and-out exploitation of natural resources by cattle barons, timber companies, mining corporations, railroads, and other entrepreneurs. By 1912, however, in a dispute as to how scarce water resources in the West should be used, the two groups of environmentalists split from each other. The division between conservationists and preservationists continues in the environmental movement to this day.

EXPLOITATION, CONSERVATION, AND PRESERVATION

Opinions on the use of our natural resources today thus take one of three directions:

Position 1. In order for our society to grow, develop, and maintain the standard of living to which we have grown accustomed, we need to explore every possible resource available to us and to exploit those which are economically feasible. For example, lumber companies should have virtually free access to the nation's forests, even in areas under government protection.

Position 2. In order to assure future generations of a standard of living comparable to our own, we need to utilize our resources very carefully, setting aside some reserves we will not use now so they will be available to our children and our children's children. Limited, carefully controlled cutting of timber should be allowed on some, if not all, public lands.

Position 3. In order to ensure that future generations have a chance to appreciate the natural world, some parts of the environment should be protected from commercial development forever. Significant portions of public land should be entirely off limits to lumbering now and at all times in the future.

In the past half century, support for conservation has become as American as apple pie. Thus, few individuals or corporations argue publicly for an aggressive program of exploitation of natural resources, as outlined in position 1 above. Still, that position is often the most attractive one financially to corporations, and it is the one American industry has followed through much of our history. In a capitalist society, this position is one that will have powerful and widespread support among business and corporate leadership and among legislators and government officials.

As our supplies of some resources diminish (for example, as we begin to run out of oil and natural gas) and as population pressures increase (for example, as demand for water and energy increase in the West), however, we may expect to hear position 2 argued more strongly by those who do want to maintain their standard of living.

Finally, as a result of those same pressures, we may anticipate that more and more individuals will shift their thinking to position 3, looking for a guarantee that nonutilitarian resources (e.g., trout streams and beautiful waterfalls) will not be swept away in a frenzy of development. The debate among those who support one or another of these three positions lies at the heart of most environmental controversies in the United States today.

THREE

THE PRICE
OF PROSPERITY

By 1970, environmental issues had become matters of great concern for many Americans. The development of an "environmental consciousness" came about as the result of dramatic changes that occurred in American society during the first half of this century. From a largely rural, technologically undeveloped nation of farmers, shopkeepers, and small businessmen, the United States grew into a primarily urban, technologically advanced, heavily industrialized society.

Americans today tend to measure the progress they have made in terms of material goods. The "good life" often means owning a nice house, one or more cars, lots of clothes, one or more television sets, a VCR, and lots of gadgets, like electric toothbrushes and trash compactors. Of course, good health care for all people, strong families, worthwhile traditions, and inspiring cultural institutions also contribute to the "good life." However, when people from other parts of the world envy the

United States, they are likely to be most impressed by our ability to own refrigerators, toasters, blue jeans, and other material goods.

The United States is not, of course, the only nation to have experienced material progress. Citizens of Canada, Japan, Australia, and many European nations have as many or even more material benefits. Because it led the way in achieving a high material standard of living, however, the U.S. continues to be a symbol—as well as a target of criticism—for all that way of life represents.

MATERIAL PROGRESS AND ENVIRONMENTAL TRADE-OFFS

By concentrating on the wonders of material progress, Americans have often ignored the environmental costs of this progress. A person driving her new convertible through the hills of southern California may not think about the environmental costs of building and using that car. Someone enjoying a vacation at a Florida beach resort may not realize the environmental damage caused by the construction of that resort. The manufacturer of a promising new hair spray may not be aware of the worldwide climatic effects to which his product may contribute.

People throughout the world have begun to recognize that material progress always has its environmental price. Every new invention, product, or development involves a trade-off. Each improvement in our standard of living is likely to result in a diminished natural environment. The development of the automotive industry is an example of the trade-offs we have had to learn to make.

From a minuscule 300 cars in the United States in 1898, vehicle registration rose to 8,000 in 1900, 2,500,000 in 1915, 9,000,000 in 1920, 20,000,000 in 1925, and 30,000,000 in 1930.[13] Automobiles quickly became one of the great success stories of modern economic and social history. Cars provided Americans with a mobility and flexibility unprecedented in human history. Henry Ford's system of mass production made it possible for millions of Americans to own cars at a reasonable cost.

The automotive industry also brought jobs and prosperity to hundreds of businesses related to the production of cars. The rapid increase in automobile production created enormous demands for iron ore, coal, rubber, and other raw materials used in the manufacture of automotive vehicles and for the petroleum products needed to operate them. Indeed, it would not be farfetched to say that the development of the U.S. automotive industry has been a critical factor in the nation's rise as one of the world's great economic powers.

Yet, from its earliest beginnings, the automotive industry has also created problems for human society and for the natural environment. Land has been torn up or set aside for the construction of roads, highways, parking lots, gasoline stations, shopping centers, motels, and other car-related purposes. Waste materials produced during the manufacture and use of cars, buses, and trucks have contributed to increasingly severe problems of air and water pollution.

In fact, a significant part of our nation's pollution problems today are a direct result of the economic success story of the automotive industry. For example, in a recent year, automotive vehicles released 46.3 million tons of carbon monoxide into the air, 33 percent of all air pollutants. They also accounted for 15 percent of all particulate matter (soot, smoke, dust, etc.), 2 percent of all sulfur oxides, 39 percent of all nitrogen oxides, and 26 percent of all volatile organic components of polluted air.[14]

The fundamental question that automotive pollution raises is similar to issues arising from other types of pollution: What amounts and kinds of environmental degradation are we willing to tolerate in exchange for any specific improvement in our standard of living? Is it worthwhile, for example, to have an increase of, say, 10 percent in carbon monoxide levels in the atmosphere if every family can have two cars rather than one?

You can probably think of similar trade-off questions. Is the warming of lakes and rivers as a result of nuclear-power-plant discharges, with possible damage to aquatic life, a fair exchange for increased amounts of electric power? Can we live with modest increases in the level of toxic wastes in the soil if that's the price of developing and producing more-efficient pesticides for agricultural use? Are we willing to destroy natural and scenic areas in order to recover valuable mineral resources such as coal, oil, and iron?

Most such environmental trade-offs can be classified into one of three general categories:

1. Those involving the production and use of energy
2. Those involving the development of new synthetic products
3. Those involving the development and use of land resources.

THE ROLE OF ENERGY
IN AMERICAN SOCIETY

One measure used by scholars to describe a country's standard of living is energy consumption, in other words the more energy the people of a nation use, the higher their quality of life. The United States, Canada, and other industrialized nations score high on standard of living by this measure. For example, the United States has only 5 percent of the world's population, but it uses nearly a third of the world's energy. In contrast, India, with 15 percent of the world's population, consumes only 1.5 percent of all its energy.[15] The typical American uses the equivalent of 9,600 kilograms (21,000 pounds) of coal each year, while the average Tanzanian uses the equivalent of only 42 kilograms (93 pounds) of coal.[16]

Prior to 1860, 80 percent of all energy used in the United States came from the burning of wood. Then, late in the nineteenth century, discoveries of coal, oil, and natural gas made these fuels (called "fossil fuels") available for our use. Since the early 1900s, nearly 90 percent of all our energy has come from these three sources.[17] We use fossil fuels to operate our cars, buses, trucks, trains, airplanes, boats, and ships; to heat and cool our homes and office buildings; to operate factories and electric-power-generating plants; and to incinerate our solid wastes. A large fraction of the coal, oil, and natural gas we burn is not utilized directly but is used in the production of our most important secondary energy source, electricity. Think for just a moment of all the ways that coal, oil, natural gas, and electricity make your life better, and perhaps

Barham Blvd
Lankershim
Ventura Blvd

"Fossil fuels": coal, oil and natural gas account for about 90 percent of energy use. Because they are "nonrenewable" resources, however, supplies will eventually become exhausted.

you can understand the connection between energy consumption and quality of life.

One problem with fossil fuels is that they are a nonrenewable resource. Unlike wood, fossil fuels are not replenished naturally after a few growing seasons. In fact, once they are used up, they are gone essentially forever. Enormous amounts of fossil fuels became available in the recent past, creating the possibility of a prosperous modern society for some parts of the world. At some time in the not too distant future, however, they will disappear because we cannot replenish them.

ENVIRONMENTAL EFFECTS OF FOSSIL FUELS

Our dependence on fossil fuels has its costs. At every step along the way—from extraction to delivery to use—our demand for fossil fuels creates environmental hazards.

Extraction and Storage of Oil

Drilling for oil and natural gas, for example, has produced environmental damage from almost the first day these fuels were discovered. Oil was thought to be so abundant in the late nineteenth century that few precautions were taken to avoid its waste. Thus, thousands or millions of barrels were lost when a new well was struck. In one case, a giant well in Lakeview, California, produced 8 million barrels in the first eighteen months of its operation, while a quarter to a half of that amount simply drained away into the environment.[18]

Containment techniques at the time also contributed to the problem. Storage tanks were not widely used until after 1900. Instead, oil was impounded in large, open lakes from which it evaporated, seeped into the ground, caught fire, or drained away.[19]

Oil companies are, of course, much more cautious in their drilling and storage practices today. Yet, accidental spills into the environment are common. For example, in January 1969 a leak developed in a newly drilled oil well off the coast of Santa Barbara, California. Approximately 48,000 liters (21,000 gallons) of oil escaped from the well daily for a period of about ten days. Birds, fish, and other animals died by the thousands, and beaches were covered with crude oil.[20]

Extraction of Coal

The search for coal also has environmental effects. Coal is obtained in one of two ways: by digging mines deep underground (subsurface mining) or by removing it from seams at or near the surface of the earth (surface or strip mining). At first glance, subsurface mining might appear to pose relatively little threat to the environment, since extraction takes place hundreds of meters below ground. Yet the error of that thinking was apparent as soon as the first coal mines were dug in Pennsylvania and Virginia in the mid-1700s.

Water passing through a subsurface mine reacts with compounds of iron and sulfur in the earth, forming sulfuric acid. The acidified water then drains into streams and rivers, producing conditions in which aquatic life cannot survive. Some streams near coal mines have become so acidic by this process they are considered "absolutely devoid of any semblance of normal aquatic life."[21] Rain-

*An offshore oil-drilling rig in
the Gulf of Mexico. Oil leaks are one
danger of this method of extraction.*

A strip-mining operation in Colorado

water washing over mine wastes on the surface also contributes to this problem.

Acidic mine drainage is a problem with surface mines as well. However, the more common complaint from environmentalists about this form of coal extraction is the damage done to landscapes. Giant power shovels can gouge out 10 to 100 cubic meters (350 to 3,500 cubic feet) of coal at a time. Critics object to the aesthetic damage that strip mining can do to the land and to the erosion that may follow strip mining. They also point out that land taken for stripping could be better used for pastureland, grazing, or some other productive activity.

Transporting Oil

The process of moving fossil fuels from their point of extraction to their place of use also involves environmental risks. Oil tankers today are the largest ships afloat. If they develop a leak or are involved in an accident, serious environmental disasters can result. For example, on March 18, 1967, a 295-m (970-foot) oil tanker, the *Torrey Canyon*, ran aground and broke apart off the coast of England. Over a period of two months the tanker lost nearly 120,000 tons of crude oil. Beaches on both the English and French sides of the English Channel were fouled with oil.[22]

Eleven years later, almost to the day, another giant tanker, the *Amoco Cadiz*, lost its steering, ran aground, and broke apart on the shore of Brittany. Over a million seabirds were killed as 220,000 tons of crude oil were discharged into the sea. Large sections of oyster farms and other fish and sea animals also died in the disaster.[23]

The most recent and largest accident of this type occurred on March 24, 1989, when the 300-meter (987-foot) tanker *Exxon Valdez* ran aground in Prince William Sound in Alaska. Nearly 44 million liters (11 million gallons) of oil were lost to the sea. The overall environmental effects of the accident may not be known for years.

Dramatic accidents like these catch the public's attention. But they probably represent only a small fraction of all the oil lost during transportation. For example, oil tankers usually carry seawater as ballast in their oil tanks. Then, when they clean out the tanks, they may simply dump the oil-water mixture into the ocean before refilling the tanks with crude oil.[24] In addition, the total effect of many small spills may be as great as that of one large spill. During just one year for which data are available (1970), more than a million tons of oil were lost in over 3,700 spills in the Western Hemisphere alone.[25]

The Combustion of Fossil Fuels

The combustion (burning) of fossil fuels also produces environmental problems. When fossil fuels burn, they produce substances that can be harmful to plants, animals (including humans), and the physical environment. These substances include those produced by (1) the incomplete combustion of fossil fuels, (2) their complete combustion, and (3) the combustion of impurities in fossil fuels.

When fossil fuels burn incompletely, they produce finely divided particles of carbon, known as particulates, and toxic carbon monoxide gas. In small concentrations, carbon monoxide causes headaches and nausea. In larger concentrations, it can produce coma and lead to death. Particulates collect in the lungs of humans and other animals, where they block respiratory passages. This condition leads to emphysema, chronic bronchitis, and other respiratory disorders.)

In this century there have been a few especially dramatic cases of air pollution. As early as December 1930, for example, the heavily industrial Meuse River valley in Belgium was struck by unusual weather conditions that, combined with heavy smoke common in the valley, resulted in nearly a hundred deaths during a three-day period.[26]

Eighteen years late, a similar disaster struck the industrial town of Donora, Pennsylvania. Twenty people died and more than half of the town's citizens became ill from the unusually heavy concentration of polluted air. In 1952, yet a third major disaster struck, this time in London. The combination of heavy industrial air pollution and a stagnant air mass over the city resulted in about 4,000 more deaths than the normal average for the period and an additional 12,000 to 15,000 excess deaths in the weeks following. Hospital admissions during the period were 40 percent greater than normal.[27]

The Greenhouse Effect

The complete combustion of fossil fuels produces carbon dioxide and water. Until quite recently, experts were not concerned about the massive release of these substances into the air. Both occur naturally and present no threat to plant or animal life. Now, however, many authorities are concerned about the possible climatic effects of carbon dioxide buildup in the atmosphere. Sunlight reflected from the earth is absorbed by carbon dioxide in the atmosphere. The more carbon dioxide in the atmosphere, the more heat the earth retains. The carbon dioxide acts much like the glass in a greenhouse, capturing and holding heat produced by sunlight.

Many scientists are now concerned that our massive use of fossil fuels has significantly increased the amount of carbon dioxide in the atmosphere. Over a period of time, they predict, this buildup of carbon dioxide will increase the earth's annual temperature. A warmer earth, in turn, may cause the melting of ice at the North and South Poles and a consequent increase in sea levels around the world. In addition to the flooding of coastal cities worldwide, higher ocean levels may also produce dramatic changes in the earth's climate. The Yukon and Northwest territories could become farmlands, while the midwestern United States might turn into a desert. The potential consequences of such a greenhouse effect are, to many scientists, the most serious risks of our heavy dependence on fossil fuels.

The possibility of a greenhouse effect illustrates the international character of many environmental problems. The accumulation of carbon dioxide in the atmosphere results largely from fossil fuel use in industrialized nations. But the greenhouse effect could well produce changes throughout the world. Egypt, Syria, Chad, Bolivia, Indonesia, and other nations that have contributed little or nothing to the carbon dioxide buildup would be likely to experience changes as serious as those in France, Canada, Japan, and other industrialized nations.

Acid Rain

Oil and coal often contain sulfur and nitrogen as impurities. When these fossil fuels burn, the sulfur and nitrogen are converted to sulfur and nitrogen oxides. These oxides then combine with water in the air to form sulfuric and nitric acids. Carried eastward by the earth's prevailing winds, the acids eventually fall to earth as acid precipitation (acid rain, acid snow, acid fog, etc.).

Many authorities now believe that acid precipitation is responsible for the destruction of plant and animal life on which it falls. Lakes in eastern Canada and the northeastern United States, for example, have become significantly more acidic in recent decades, and organisms living in those lakes have died as a result. Acid rain may also be responsible for the destruction of large stretches of forests in these same regions.

Acid precipitation provides another example of the international nature of environmental problems. As far back as a century ago, Norway and Sweden were experiencing the environmental effects of acid rain on their lakes and forests. At that time, the damage resulted from industrial activity in the British midlands. Sulfuric and nitric acid produced in the smoke of English factories were carried by prevailing winds across the North Sea and deposited across Scandinavia. Thus, while environmental problems are of local, state, and national concern, many—like the greenhouse effect and acid rain—involve many nations and often the whole world community.

Alternative Sources of Energy

The fundamental issue that our society faces, then, is how much damage to the environment we are willing to tolerate in exchange for the high quality of life that our intensive use of energy has made possible. If we choose to fight against the proposed

Aerial view of the Davis-Besse Nuclear Power Station in Ohio. Although nuclear energy is an alternative to the use of fossil fuels, many environmentalists believe the dangers outweigh the benefits.

offshore oil drilling near our home, are we willing to pay more on our energy bills next year or, perhaps, give up entirely our electric hair dryer or the use of our car for one day a week? Nearly all environmental questions involve choices such as these: If we don't want further damage to the environment, what conveniences are we willing to give up?

Some people want it both ways. They believe we can have a strong, growing economy, as we have had for nearly a century, without degrading the environment any further. We can do that, they suggest, by looking for alternative sources of energy: nuclear, geothermal, and solar power, for example. One problem with this approach, however, is that those who worry about environmental damage tend to oppose the use of nuclear power plants also. The potential environmental threat of hundreds of such plants may be even worse, they believe, than the environmental problems with which we now live.

As a result of this fear, opposition to and constraints on nuclear power plants have become so severe that only two new orders for nuclear power plants were placed in the decade following 1978, and eighty-four previous orders were canceled during the same time.[28]

The final alternatives, then, involve the development of some energy resources essentially unused today: solar energy or fusion power, for example. Research during the 1970s began to examine ways in which these alternative sources could begin to replace fossil fuels as suppliers of our nation's energy needs. Such research diminished considerably, however, in the 1980s. A combination of reduced oil prices and lack of interest by the Reagan administration reduced funds available to

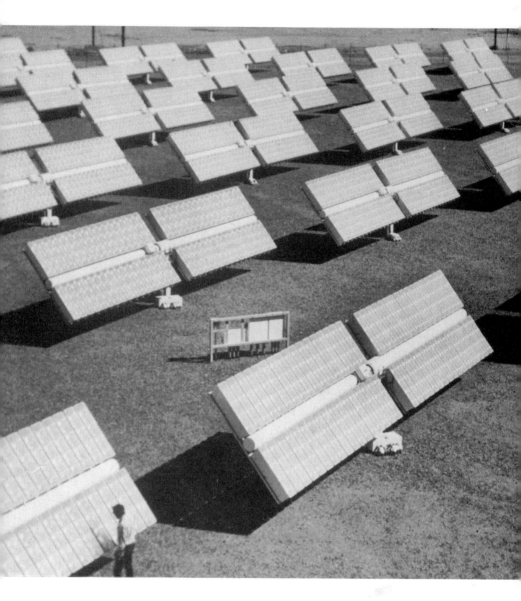

*A large solar-cell power plant
in Arizona. Scale is shown by the
man standing at lower left.*

Wind turbines are another
alternative energy source.

support research on alternative energy sources. As the 1980s drew to a close, little effort was being made to find and develop options to fossil fuels and nuclear power and the environmental problems they present.[29]

ENVIRONMENTAL PROBLEMS FROM SYNTHETIC PRODUCTS

A second set of environmental issues we face involves the production and use of synthetic substances. The vast majority of medicines, cosmetics, dyes, rubber, paints, pesticides and herbicides, and all plastics are synthetic materials produced by the endless imagination of chemical researchers. These products have made our lives healthier, safer, richer, and more interesting. It is hard to imagine what our lives would be like, in fact, without synthetic products such as buffered aspirin, nylon, latex-base paints, suntan oils, synthetic detergents, lipsticks, anticaking agents in foods, anticancer drugs, insecticides, vinyl phonograph records, transistors, gasoline additives, and thousands of other products of major and minor significance. Wonders of chemical research such as these have made American society the envy of the world.

Yet, the principle we learned in dealing with energy issues—that almost all forms of "progress" come at some price to pay—holds true for synthetic chemical products also. We could show how the development of virtually every item listed in the paragraph above has created new problems for humans and/or for the environment. A group of synthetic compounds known as the polychlorinated biphenyls illustrate this point.

PCBs

The polychlorinated biphenyls (PCBs) are a group of organic compounds first invented in the 1930s. They have a number of desirable chemical and physical properties and have been put to use by industry in the manufacture of many products, including paints, varnishes, sealants, plastic coatings, tires, soaps, ceramics, glass, brake linings, and grinding wheels. Their most important application has been as a heat-exchange and insulating material in electrical equipment.

PCBs constitute a problem for the environment in two ways, however. First, they are extremely toxic. Very low levels of PCB have been shown to cause health problems such as growth retardation and stillbirths in humans, and central-nervous-system and eye defects in other animals. The U.S. Food and Drug Administration (FDA) has set 2 parts per million (ppm) as the highest acceptable concentration of PCBs in fish to be eaten by humans.

Second, PCBs are very stable. In fact, their stability is one reason they are so attractive to industry. They do not break down even when exposed to extreme conditions of heat, pressure, or severe weather conditions. But that also means the PCBs that escape into the environment will be around for a very long time. This combination of properties—toxicity and persistence—makes the PCBs a serious environmental hazard.

By the late 1960s, reports were beginning to appear of PCB poisonings in various parts of the world. In 1968, for example, rice oil in Japan that was contaminated with PCBs caused eye infections, acne, jaundice, swelling of joints, liver disease, and other health problems among those who had used the oil.

By the 1970s, a more serious problem became obvious. PCBs lost during the manufacturing process and escaping from products that contained them were leaking into the environment. Surveys by governmental agencies found unacceptably high concentrations of PCBs in the Great Lakes, the Ohio River, and other inland waterways. In one 1976 study, for example, 98.1 percent of all individuals examined were found to have at least some PCBs in their bodies. Nearly 60 percent had 1 ppm, 29 percent had 1 to 3 ppm, and 9 percent had more than 3 ppm.[30]

By 1978, the Environmental Protection Agency (EPA) had become convinced that PCBs presented a serious environmental hazard and banned their use in all but closed systems and, in 1979, in all applications. The government had concluded that the many benefits offered by PCBs simply did not justify the environmental hazard they posed.

Looking back, the issue presented by PCBs is a fairly simple one. These compounds did offer great benefits to industry, but their threat to human health was just too great to permit their use. The problems posed by most other synthetic chemicals are less clear and less simple. The insecticide DDT was banned for most uses in the United States in 1972, for example, because of its danger to birds, fish, and other animal life in the environment. Yet its use in many parts of the world has saved untold numbers of human lives by preventing the spread of malaria.[31] Balancing the enormous human health benefits of DDT against its terrible threat to many forms of wildlife is a difficult challenge. Questions such as these about the relative benefits and risks of synthetic chemicals are often difficult to resolve.

ENVIRONMENTAL PROBLEMS INVOLVING DEVELOPMENT

The third area in which environmental disputes arise involves land and water use. If you have ever flown from coast to coast across the United States or Canada, you might wonder how land use could be a problem in either country. Certainly there is more land than our populations could possibly use in the foreseeable future.

The problem is that some lands are more desirable than others. For example, people often prefer to live near the water. More than half of the people in the United States live along an Atlantic, Pacific, Gulf Coast, or Great Lakes coastline, and the population in these areas is growing three times as fast as the national rate.[32] Ocean and waterfront property are at high priority. People want to build homes, office buildings and shopping centers close to water.

In addition, people tend to prefer living in and near cities rather than in the country. The average population density is about 64 people per square mile in the United States, and about 6 people per square mile in Canada. Yet, the population density in urban areas in both countries is much greater, about 2,500 people per square mile.[33]

In addition, the land on which people want to build is often environmentally important. For example, salt and freshwater marshes, swamps, and other kinds of wetlands often occupy the very sites that humans want for development. Since these wetlands appear to be empty and useless, developers tend not to worry about filling them in and building on top of them.

As a result, at least 50 percent of the nation's original wetlands have been altered or destroyed. Between the mid-1950s and mid-1970s, the loss of wetlands amounted to about 500,000 acres (about 200,000 hectares) per year. In the last decade, that rate has been reduced somewhat (largely because of new legislation), but still runs at about 300,000 acres (about 120,000 hectares) per year.[34]

Ecologically, however, wetlands are neither empty nor useless. In fact, they constitute one of the most biologically productive of all areas in the environment. The wetlands provide natural habitats for a great variety of plants and animals, many of which find their way into the oceans during the mature stages of their life cycles. By some estimates, for example, two-thirds of all commercially important fish and shellfish taken along the Atlantic coast and the Gulf of Mexico and half of those taken along the Pacific coast use coastal wetlands for their feeding and spawning.[35]

In other cases, the controversy over land use goes beyond monetary values. The growth of urban areas in southern California, for example, has created enormous demands for fresh water. One way of meeting these demands has been to dam rivers and draw from lakes in northern California, Nevada, and other states. But for many people, these lakes and rivers are an important recreational resource. They provide opportunities for fishing, rafting, swimming, and just being close to nature. In these cases, the debate becomes one between

Wetlands are a natural habitat for many kinds of plants and animals. They are often also commercially desirable, however, and environmentalists have fought many battles over their use.

meeting the water needs of a growing urban area and preserving at least some parts of the environment in its natural, pristine character.

Issues in contemporary America such as these reflect environmental controversies that go back more than a century. What trade-offs are we willing to accept in the environment? Will we be satisfied to live a simpler, less energy-intensive life in exchange for a clear view off the Mendocino coast, with no oil rigs in sight? Or is a less appealing view of the ocean a fair exchange for a more comfortable lifestyle?

Is a modest increase in the rate of stillborn and deformed wildlife a reasonable price to pay for a long-lasting house paint, a highly effective pesticide, or a truly wrinkle-free fabric? Or can we live with the commercial products we have, or even less desirable forms of them, in order to keep the environment safe from harm? People take different stands on questions such as these. And those differences of opinion make for the environmental debates that have raged throughout the United States and Canada in the last third of the twentieth century.

FOUR

HEROES AND HEROINES OF THE ENVIRONMENTAL MOVEMENT

The fight to protect our environment has had its heroes and heroines in nearly every period of American history. Whenever corporate raiders or governmental agencies or individual robber barons threatened our natural resources, men and women stood up to these challenges and did what they could to protect the environment.

In the first two centuries of our nation's existence, the voices of environmental defense were relatively few and far between. The notion that farmers, miners, lumbermen, and others who used our natural resources should think about preservation and conservation was simply unheard of and unimagined by the nation's leaders.

ROOTS OF AN AMERICAN ENVIRONMENTAL MOVEMENT

To be sure, exceptions to this philosophy existed. President John Quincy Adams, for example, was outraged at congressional giveaways of public land to speculators.[36] But nothing that could be regarded as an environmental movement began to appear until well into the nineteenth century. Among the still small number of individuals who fostered that movement were Henry David Thoreau and George Perkins Marsh.

Henry David Thoreau

Thoreau's contribution to the environmental movement was an attitude toward the natural world that stood in marked contrast to that of most of his contemporaries. It was a philosophy of nature that would inspire and reappear in the lives of later environmental leaders like John Muir, Aldo Leopold, Joseph Wood Krutch, Olaus Murie, and William O. Douglas.

Probably the most famous episode of Thoreau's life was the nearly two-year period he spent at Walden Pond. On land donated by his friend and mentor, Ralph Waldo Emerson, Thoreau built a small house, planted a garden, and settled down to a simple, contemplative life. Two books, *A Week on the Concord and Merrimack Rivers* and *Walden, or Life in the Woods,* resulted from this experience.

Henry David Thoreau (1817– 1862). Thoreau's writings, especially Walden, *have been a source of inspiration to many environmentalists.*

In these books and his later writings, Thoreau outlined his philosophy of nature and the relationship of women and men to it. Thoreau believed that nature was the source of spiritual truth and moral law. He wrote "there is a subtle magnetism in Nature, which, if we unconsciously yield to it, will direct us aright."[37]

Thoreau regarded nature as a critical antidote to the commercial and industrialized society he saw growing up around him. All that saved humans from the madness of "progress," he felt, was the wilderness that still surrounded cities and towns. Nature provided a healthy, inspirational, and motivating force.

Thoreau believed this force had gone out of the lives of city dwellers, leaving them with "lives of quiet desperation." Thoreau was also a realist, however, and saw that most humans "do not care for Nature and would sell their share in all her beauty, as long as they may live, for a stated sum—many for a glass of rum."[38]

Thoreau's influence on later environmentalists arose from his passionate writings. He was not a political activist, and the only cause attracting his actual participation was the antislavery abolitionist movement of the mid-1800s.

George Perkins Marsh

The role played by George Perkins Marsh in the early environmental movement was quite different from that of Thoreau. Marsh was a lawyer who spent most of his life in government service. He was U.S. minister to Turkey from 1849 to 1854 and minister to Italy from 1861 to 1882. Marsh wrote not about the philosophical, mystical, almost religious value of nature, but, in much more concrete terms, about the interrelationship of nature and human societies.

Although not a scientist, Marsh was very conscious of the impact of human societies on their environment. As a boy in Vermont, he witnessed extensive erosion caused by careless logging and agricultural practices. In Europe, he studied in great detail the devastation that early and modern societies had made and were still making on the landscape. He concluded that all human activity caused serious damage to the environment, and that environmental damage, in turn, was instrumental in the fall of many civilizations.

Marsh's monumental book, *Man and Nature, or Physical Geography as Modified by Human Action,* argued that the capability humans have to alter their environment carries with it an implicit obligation to do so responsibly. Ignoring that responsibility, Marsh felt, constituted a serious threat to a nation's survival.

More than half of *Man and Nature* dealt with the importance of forests in soil and water conservation. Some of the suggestions he made for conserving and protecting land and forests have been called a "harbinger of regional reclamation efforts such as that involving the Tennessee valley."[39] And the final chapter, on the potential environmental effects of the proposed Suez Canal, has been described as "the first environmental impact report."[40]

CONSERVATIONISTS AND PRESERVATIONISTS

The philosophy of "use up and move on" was virtually unchallenged in the United States as long as new lands remained to be conquered. By the 1880s, that situation no longer existed. The Western Frontier had reached the Pacific Ocean. For the first time, thoughtful men and women began to think about the environmental consequences of the way Americans were using their land. Some, the conservationists, suggested using our natural resources more carefully so that they would last far into the future. Others, the preservationists, recommended that at least some resources be placed "off limits," protecting them from exploitation forever. These two views are reflected in the lives of Gifford Pinchot and John Muir.

Gifford Pinchot

Gifford Pinchot came from a wealthy Pennsylvania family with a strong social conscience. In his early years Gifford was taught to recognize and care about social injustice. This training had its effects later in life when as head of the National Forest Service he surprised colleagues by appointing women and blacks to positions of authority. Such

Gifford Pinchot, who headed the Division of Forestry in the U.S. Department of Agriculture, was a leading voice in the movement for a "multiple use, sustained yield" philosophy of resource management.

appointments were considered by most people to be revolutionary at that time in American history.

Pinchot's choice of careers was influenced by his father's concern about the nation's loss of its forests. The elder Pinchot encouraged his son to consider a professional career in forestry, an occupation that did not even exist in the United States at the time.

After graduation from Yale University in 1889, Pinchot spent thirteen months at the French Forest School in Nancy. Upon his return to the United States, he worked as a consulting forester. His most important assignment was the construction of a demonstration forest at George W. Vanderbilt's Biltmore estate at Asheville, North Carolina. In 1898 he was appointed Chief of the Division of Forestry in the Department of Agriculture, a position he held until 1910.

Pinchot's extensive work in the Division of Forestry (later called the Bureau of Forestry and later still, the National Forest Service) was directed by a philosophy of conservation. Unlike Thoreau, he did not think of trees in terms of the inspiration they could bring humans, but as an economic asset. It was essential, he believed, to manage the nation's timber resources carefully so that they could be harvested profitably *and* conserved for use by future generations.

Pinchot was an early proponent of the "multiple use, sustained yield" philosophy. He proposed that forest lands be managed scientifically so that they could be used for lumbering, grazing, agricultural production, and exploitation of water resources. The purpose of careful management was to ensure that the largest possible yield could be obtained from all these activities now and into the future.

Pinchot achieved much because of his aggressive, forceful personality. Throughout his career, he traveled around the nation, lecturing and teaching about forest conservation, writing letters and pamphlets, organizing support groups, contacting newspapers, lobbying other government officials, and donating money to schools and colleges. One of the most difficult of his tasks was to persuade lumbermen, ranchers, miners, and settlers in the West to think about their natural resources in an entirely new way.

John Muir

Pinchot's activities were similar to those to his somewhat older contemporary, John Muir. Muir was born in Scotland in 1838 and brought up in Wisconsin. After two and a half years at the University of Wisconsin, he set out to walk from Indianapolis to the Gulf of Mexico, a trip he later described in *A Thousand-Mile Walk to the Gulf* (1916).

Muir's walk was motivated by his desire to live in the wilderness and to learn more about nature. By 1868, that drive had taken him to California, where he settled in the Yosemite Valley. There he was able to devote his time to the study of trees, flowers, forests, glaciers, and other aspects of the environment at his leisure. When he needed money he worked (at first) at a nearby sheep ranch or sawmill or (later) as a nature guide or writer.

On his guiding expeditions he made contacts with many important scientific and political figures (Teddy Roosevelt was perhaps the most important), whose friendship would later be valuable in his ef-

1903

forts to preserve natural resources. But it was through his articles in magazines like *The National Geographic, Harper's,* and *Overland Monthly* and his books like *The Mountains of California, Our National Parks, Travels in Alaska, The Yosemite,* and *Steep Trails* that Muir brought his philosophy of nature to millions throughout the nation and the world.

Muir's message to the public was one of preservation. Unlike Pinchot, he did not argue for more efficient logging or grazing or mining techniques, but for protection of the environment from the onslaught of human "progress." Like Thoreau, Muir thought that "wilderness mirrors divinity, nourishes humanity, and vivifies the spirit."[41] He was convinced that "a heart like our own must be beating in every crystal and cell" of the wilderness around him.[42] He used the power of his pen to plead for the protection of the wilderness from the attacks of industry. The following passage reflects the passion with which he could present the case for preservation:

John Muir (left), whose efforts were instrumental in the creation of our first national parks, shown here with Theodore Roosevelt. As president, Roosevelt was a strong supporter of measures to protect the environment.

Any fool can destroy trees. They cannot run away; and if they could, they would still be destroyed—chased and hunted down as long as fun or a dollar could be got out of their bark hides. . . . Through all the wonderful, eventful centuries since Christ's time—and long before that—God has cared for these trees, saved them from drought, disease, avalanches, and a thousand straining, leveling tempests and floods; but he cannot save them from fools—only Uncle Sam can do that.[43]

Muir was one of the founding members of the Sierra Club in 1892. The club was organized in order to "explore, enjoy, and render accessible the mountain regions of the Pacific Coast" and "to enlist the support and co-operation of the people and the government in preserving the forests and other natural features of the Sierra Nevada mountains."[44]

Muir was instrumental in achieving some major environmental victories including the passage of bills that created Yosemite, Sequoia, and General Grant National Parks and that allowed the president to create forest preserves from public lands. Acting under the latter law, President Benjamin Harrison set aside 13,000,000 acres (about 5,260,000 hectares) of land in 1891 as the nation's first forest preserves.[45]

Muir lost the last great environmental battle of his life, however, and lost it to his longtime friend and ally, Gifford Pinchot. The battle concerned the proposed damming of the beautiful Hetch Hetchy Valley, 15 miles (24 km) northwest of Yosemite Valley. The Hetch Hetchy dam was designed to provide the city of San Francisco with a dependable water supply, an objective that was consistent with Pinchot's philosophy of wise use of water resources, but at odds with Muir's belief in the preservation of natural areas of unusual beauty. The Hetch Hetchy issue not only became a professional disagreement between Muir and Pinchot, but also turned into a bitter personal feud between the two environmentalists.[46] After a long and bitter battle, the U.S. Congress approved the Hetch Hetchy plan in 1913. Muir died a year later.

THE ENVIRONMENTAL MOVEMENT IN THE TWENTIETH CENTURY

Battles over the environment have become an everyday part of life in the United States today. Sometimes those battles are waged by individuals who see a cause and devote their time and energy to speaking out for conservation or preservation. More often today, environmental causes are championed by formal organizations consisting of hundreds or thousands of men and women whose names we will never know or have long forgotten. John Muir's Sierra Club (1892) and Aldo Leopold's Wilderness Society (1935) are classic examples of these organizations.

By the 1970s, a growing national environmental consciousness had spawned dozens of national and hundreds of regional, state, and local organizations. The appendix lists a number of these organizations.

Rachel Carson

When did Americans first develop an "environmental consciousness"? It's impossible to give a simple answer to that question. But a critical milestone in attracting our attention to the world's environmental problems was certainly the publication of Rachel Carson's *Silent Spring* in 1962.

Carson was born in Springdale, Pennsylvania, on May 27, 1907. Throughout her life, she combined two passions—a love of literature and a concern about the living world. Her first literary accomplishment came at the age of ten years when *St. Nicholas* magazine accepted one of her stories for publication. For a time it seemed that writing would become her career.

Carson's plans were altered during her sophomore year at the Pennsylvania College for Women. There an introductory course in biology inspired her to major in zoology. Eventually she went on to Johns Hopkins University to earn a master's degree in genetics. From that time on, Carson found ways to combine her love of writing and of nature. Her first job, for example, was with the U.S. Bureau of

Rachel Carson (1907–1964), scientist and writer. Her influential book Silent Spring, *published in 1962, called attention to the harmful effects of pesticides on wildlife.*

Fisheries in Washington, D.C., where among other things she wrote scripts for a series of radio broadcasts entitled "Romance under the Waters."

Carson's life was dogged by misfortune. Her father died when she was twenty-eight, forcing her to assume part of the family's financial burden. A year later, her older sister died, and Rachel become the sole source of support for her sister's two children. Still later, a niece died, leaving another young child for Rachel to raise.

Meanwhile Carson's own health was really not adequate to sustain all these responsibilities. As she grew older she developed arthritis, an ulcer, and a sensitivity to staph infections. Finally she developed cancer, from which she died on April 14, 1964.

All of these burdens did not prevent Carson from leaving a brilliant literary legacy. Even had she not written her most famous book, *Silent Spring*, she would still be revered for her trilogy about the sea: *The Sea Around Us, Under the Sea-Wind,* and *The Edge of the Sea.* But Rachel Carson's name will probably always be remembered in connection with *Silent Spring*.

By the late 1950s, observers of nature were noticing dramatic changes in animal populations. Birds that once could be seen in abundance appeared to be vanishing. Fewer eggs were hatching, and among those that did, a larger than normal fraction of fledglings were dying. Carson and other biologists were convinced that the extensive use of pesticides was a major factor in this change. She decided to search out what was known about pesticides and their effects on plants and animals.

Her research took four years. In 1962 she completed *Silent Spring*, which pointed out the way in which thoughtless use of pesticides was damaging the environment. She argued against the prevailing wisdom that synthetic pesticides—especially the chlorinated hydrocarbons—were an unalloyed blessing to human civilization. She thought that such pesticides should be used sparingly and only with the greatest caution.

The "silent spring" that gave the book its title was Carson's image of the worst possible future for the world, in which overuse of pesticides had killed off birds and other animals. In such a world, she believed, spring would come unannounced by the songs of birds or the sounds of other animals.

Carson's message was not received enthusiastically by many segments of society. Some professional scientists, for example, felt that she did not have the academic qualifications to make the judgments expressed in *Silent Spring*. Public-health workers feared that the book would restrict the use of chemicals such as DDT, which had already saved untold millions of human lives by curbing the spread of malaria. And chemical manufacturers were naturally concerned about the financial impact that Carson's book would have on their businesses.

Now, more than twenty-five years after the publication of *Silent Spring*, we can make a better judgment about Rachel Carson and her contribution to the environmental movement. Carson was never an aggressive environmental activist. She did not lead marches, organize sit-ins, or fight at the forefront of the environmental movement. She was much too quiet and reclusive, a woman who was not eager to enter into acrimonious public debates with her critics. She prepared her case with careful research and presented her arguments thoughtfully and clearly.

No doubt *Silent Spring* contains some strong points and some weak ones, some important facts and some inaccuracies. Yet Rachel Carson's contribution to the environmental movement probably lies not so much in the specific details of her book as in the overall message the book conveys. As one observer has written, she laid out for the general public

> the concept of ecology; the way the natural world fits together, the pieces so tightly and inextricably bound that you could not isolate cause and effect. The consequences of any action rippled through the whole system, affecting everything and sometimes even changing the system itself.[47]

Environmental Organizations

Environmental organizations face problems that individual activists don't worry about. For example, an environmental organization has to consider the philosophies, expectations, objectives, and strategies of many individuals. And the longer that organization has been in existence, the more likely it is that these philosophies, expectations, objectives, and strategies will diverge within the organization and away from its original program. The Sierra Club is a case in point.

The Sierra Club had been formed in San Francisco by John Muir and his colleagues partly as an organization for political activism and partly as a social, nature, and hiking club for relatively well-to-do Californians. After Muir's death, however, club members became more interested in social activities than in environmental issues. As one environmental historian has pointed out, "The Sierra Club had not won a single major environmental issue in the thirty-eight years since Muir's death" until a new executive director, David Brower, was appointed in 1952.[48]

Brower was one of the most progressive environmentalists in the United States when he was chosen executive director of the club. He brought a new philosophy of environmental activism to the Sierra Club during his seventeen-year tenure as executive director.

Club membership increased under his leadership from seven thousand to seventy-seven thousand during that period. Many of the new members (85 percent according to one poll[49]) were recruited by Brower's philosophy and saw political activism as a legitimate role for the club.

The pace of political activity quickened during the 1960s as the Sierra Club took out full-page ads on environmental issues in major newspapers across the land, began a large and aggressive book-publishing division, and encouraged its members to make their views known in every possible form of political protest. A classic example of this approach was a series of seven "Battlebooks," published by the club, that taught citizens exactly how to become active in environmental issues such as wilderness preservation.[50]

By the mid-1960s, however, club directors were becoming increasingly concerned about what seemed to them to be the freewheeling, deficit-spending approach Brower had adopted.[51] Finally, at a board of directors' meeting on May 3, 1969,

Brower was fired as executive director of the Sierra Club.

Brower's environmental work did not end with his firing, however. Three months later he had obtained a grant to organize the John Muir Institute, a foundation devoted to environmental education. Before the end of the year, Brower had created his own environmental organization, Friends of the Earth. Friends of the Earth continues the strong activist philosophy of Brower's work at the Sierra Club, lobbying for better environmental protection and initiating lawsuits to protect the environment.

Interestingly enough, the direction set by Brower for the Sierra Club did not change after his departure. The club continues to be at the forefront of most environmental battles in the United States. The club's 1987 platform illustrates how its initial objectives have been broadened to include a wide range of issues affecting the environment. That platform lists six "national conservation campaigns" for the club during the year: Clean Air Act reauthorization; Arctic National Wildlife Refuge protection; Bureau of Land Management Wilderness/ Desert National Parks identification; National Forests/National Parks protection; Implementation of toxic controls laws; and onshore oil and gas leasing/high-level nuclear waste programs.[52]

ENVIRONMENTAL LEADERS IN GOVERNMENT

Environmental issues are sometimes seen as battles between "the people" and governmental agencies. Although the record shows this has often been the case, some of the greatest environmental triumphs in American history have come as the result of action by governmental leaders.

Among the greatest of all environmental champions, for example, was President Theodore Roosevelt. Roosevelt's two-term presidency has been called "the zenith of Progressive conservation."[53] It was through Roosevelt's support that Gifford Pinchot was able to achieve most of the accomplishments that marked the Chief Forester's distinguished career.

In recent years, the lives of William O. Douglas and Stewart Udall have further illustrated the role that governmental officials can play in the environmental movement.

William O. Douglas

Douglas was born in 1898, suffered from polio at the age of three, and, like many other polio victims, turned to outdoor exercise as a way of compensating for the physical damage done to his body by the disease. His early years were spent in hiking, running, and camping in the wilderness areas around his home in Yakima, Washington. His devotion to nature continued throughout his life, even after his appointment as justice of the Supreme Court in 1939.

Each vacation found Justice Douglas on a new journey of adventure: horseback riding in the Cascades, fishing on the Columbia River, walking the woods around Washington, or hiking in the Himalayas. Many of his nearly thirty books deal with environmental topics. Among these are *Of Men and Mountains* (1950), *Beyond the High Himalayas* (1952), *North from Malaya* (1953), and *The Pacific West* (1961).

For Justice Douglas, the environment was not just a source of inspiration and recreation during his vacation times. It was a central issue in many legal cases he decided. Probably the most crucial of these cases, decided by the Supreme Court in 1972, involved the proposed construction of a huge ski resort in the Mineral King Valley of Sequoia National Forest by Walt Disney Enterprises.

Worried about the potential environmental damage of this project, the Sierra Club sued to stop construction of the resort. Disney responded by saying that the Sierra Club had no "standing" in the case, that is, owned no property in the area and therefore had no cause to become involved in the case. The Supreme Court agreed with Disney, but the case is probably best remembered because of Justice Douglas's dissenting opinion.

In that opinion, Douglas argued, in essence, that "rocks have rights too." He wrote that "valleys, alpine meadows, rivers, lakes, estuaries, beaches, ridges, groves of trees, swampland, or even air [feel] the destructive pressures of modern technology and modern life." He then argued that the Sierra Club *did* have standing in the case.

Supreme Court Justice William O. Douglas (1898–1980) was a strong advocate of environmental preservation. Here he is engaged in one of his favorite pastimes, hiking.

Those who hike [the environment], hunt it, camp on it, or frequent it, or visit it merely to sit in solitude and wonderment are legitimate spokesmen for it, whether they be few or many. Those who have that intimate relation with the inanimate object to be injured, polluted, or otherwise despoiled are its legitimate spokesmen.[54]

Douglas's opinion was in the minority when that philosophy was expressed. In the twenty years since, however, the argument has won more and more converts and seems to be gaining acceptance as a legitimate principle in environmental law.

Stewart Udall

Stewart Udall was born in St. John's, Arizona, in 1920. He was elected to Congress from the state's Second District in 1954. In 1961, he was chosen for the post of secretary of the interior by President John F. Kennedy. Udall remained in that position for eight years, serving under both presidents Kennedy and Johnson.

One might expect the secretary of the interior to be an aggressive environmental activist. After all, the Interior Department is responsible for managing about 70 percent of all federally owned land in the United States, one-third of the nation's total land area.[55] If the secretary of the interior is not an ardent conservationist or preservationist, then who will be?

Yet, the Interior Department has often acted more aggressively in the interests of those it is supposed to manage (lumber, mining, and power companies, for example) than in the interests of the general public.[56] Secretary Udall was not, however, made in that mold. His record demonstrates a sincere and continuous concern for the quality of the American environment.

During his tenure as interior secretary, Udall added four new national parks, two new national recreation areas, and six new national seashores. In addition, his efforts convinced the Congress to establish the National Seashores System, the Wild and Scenic Rivers System, and the National Wilderness Preservation System.[57]

Secretary Udall's philosophy is brought together in his book *The Quiet Crisis,* published in 1963. Udall describes the conditions that had created an environmental crisis in the United States of the 1960s, the trade-offs the nation faces, and the reasons that Americans had cause to hope for the future. He pointed out that

> *we can produce a wide range of goods and machines, but our manipulations have multiplied waste products that befoul the land, and have introduced frightening new forms of erosion that diminish the quality of indispensable resources and even imperil human health.*[58]

Udall's hope for resolving the environmental crisis was to remind us of how an earlier environmentalist would view our present situation and describe the options confronting us:

> *Henry Thoreau would scoff at the notion that the Gross National Product should be the chief index to the state of the nation, or that automobile sales or figures on consumer consumption reveal anything significant about the authentic*

art of living. . . . To those who complain of the complexity of modern life, he might reply, "If you want inner peace find it in solitude, not speed, and if you would find yourself, look to the land from which you came and to which you go.[59]

For leaders of the environmental movement in our own era, no less than for Stewart Udall, the issues and choices present at our nation's birth have remained with us ever since. They are still challenging us in the last decades of the twentieth century.

The Environmental Activist
Next Door: Lois Gibbs

The environmental movement is nothing if not democratic. The Muirs and Browers of this world would have achieved little had they not been able to call on bookkeepers, homemakers, teachers, librarians, students, and other volunteers from every walk of life, volunteers who wrote letters, donated money, stuffed envelopes, collected names on petitions, and served in untold numbers of other ways.

Typical of that person-next-door who has kept the environmental movement alive in the United States for three hundred years is Lois Gibbs. Environmental issues had no place in the first twenty-five years of Ms. Gibbs's life. In 1977 she was living in a three-bedroom ranch home in Niagara Falls, New York, with her husband and their two children. She was so typical that her mother had once referred to her as "Susie Homemaker."[60] But the events of the next few years were to dramatically alter Ms. Gibbs's life.

In late 1977, her son, Michael, began having epileptic seizures. The first seizures occurred at just about the time the local newspaper was carrying a series of articles on toxic wastes that had been buried under land on which Michael's school had been built. More than two decades earlier, the wastes had been dumped into the 1-kilometer-long (0.6 mile) Love Canal and then covered over by the Hooker Chemical Company.

At the time, residents knew little or nothing about the nature of these chemical wastes. Nor had any definite connection between these wastes and health effects been demonstrated. Still, Ms. Gibbs was convinced that the long-buried toxic wastes were responsible for her son's health problems. She set out to convince city officials that the school should be closed. Her door-to-door campaign produced a petition signed by 161 residents of the area. Although the city agreed to close the school, the petitioners were still not satisfied. They formed the Love Canal Homeowners Association to obtain assistance from the state and federal governments. Ms. Gibbs was elected president of the association.

Actions of the Homeowners Association were instrumental in persuading the federal government to declare the Love Canal area a federal disaster area. By 1980, more than $30 million had been spent to clean up the toxic-waste site, and another $35 million had been used to move nearly six hundred families from a 70-acre site around the canal.[61]

After the Love Canal battle was over, Ms. Gibbs moved to Virginia, where she continued to appear on radio and television and to give lectures in which she described her own role as an environmental activist. Her autobiography, *Love Canal, My Story,* and a 1982 television documentary, "Lois Gibbs and the Love Canal," have also told the story of how a single person aroused by a vital environmental issue can make a real difference in her own community. In recent years, Ms. Gibbs has founded a nationally important environmental organization, the Citizens Clearinghouse for Hazardous Wastes, of which she is now executive director.

FIVE

YOUNG
ENVIRONMENTAL
ACTIVISTS

In Chapter Four we saw that not only famous men and women but also "people next door" like Lois Gibbs can help achieve significant victories in the environmental movement. Environmental heroes and heroines can be found in many places, perhaps in your own town or your own school. They include people like Bill Buck, profiled in Chapter One. Here are other stories of young women and men, not so different from you, who have made a difference in the environmental movement.

PROTECTING THE OCEANS
OFF CALIFORNIA:
MEADOW MAKOVKIN

Making a difference is what Meadow Makovkin's life has been all about. At the time of her graduation from Mendocino (California) High School in 1988, Meadow had attained some degree of fame for her part in the Ocean Sanctuary Movement in northern California. Ocean Sanctuary is an organization created to fight plans for oil drilling in the Pacific Coast, off the coast of Mendocino and Humboldt counties.

In 1987, the U.S. Interior Department had announced plans for Lease Sale 91, a program under which oil companies would be allowed to explore for oil under the continental shelf, off the coast of California from San Diego to the Oregon border. In Mendocino and Humboldt counties alone, as many as twenty-two oil drilling platforms would have been erected, each platform serving between fifty and eighty individual wells. Pipelines on the ocean floor would have connected drilling platforms to oil- and gas-processing plants either on- or offshore.[62]

Representatives of the Department of the Interior and the oil companies argued that the platforms represented no threat to the environment. Rogge Marsh, of Exxon, pointed out that "We've been shooting oil in the Gulf of Mexico for years, and as far as we know there's no significant change to the fish population or the mammals out there."[63]

Residents of the largely rural, scenic counties did not see things quite that way. They argued that drilling for oil off the coast would cause irreparable damage to the environment, disturbing whales, seals, porpoises, fish populations, and the tranquil life people sought in that remote part of the state. Most people in Mendocino and Humboldt counties are protective of the pristine beauty of their environment, and are not willing to give up their fight easily.[64]

Meadow remembers the precise moment when she became interested in the anti–oil-drilling battle, soon to be called Ocean Sanctuary. When a fellow high school student remarked to her, "You know, that could really happen," she decided it was time for her to get busy and do something. Her first step was to prepare a brief statement to present during an Interior Department hearing held in Mendocino County. Next, she showed up at the Mendocino office of Ocean Sanctuary and volunteered to do "whatever needed to be done" for the organization.

Meadow immediately discovered a fact of life with volunteer work. Formal structure and organization may be scanty. "Everyone works together," she points out, "inventing his or her responsibilities. A person can be intimidated by an apparent lack of direction, but must be resourceful and imaginative in creating his or her own jobs."

Some of Meadow's tasks were modest: photocopying testimony, helping out at a benefit concert, and operating an information table in downtown Mendocino. Later, she was asked to take on other assignments. She spoke at a rally for presidential candidate Jesse Jackson and was asked to speak before the Governmental Organizations Committee (GOC) of the State Senate in the state capitol at Sacramento. Her GOC appearance was broadcast on a national television newscast.

Perhaps most important of all, Meadow is a living, breathing advertisement for the principles of environmental activism. She takes and makes every opportunity to let other teenagers and adults know what the issues are, what is at stake, and what needs to be done to protect the environment. She has presented the case for Ocean Sanctuary informally around school, in class presentations and school assemblies, and in interschool conferences. She points out that the simple act of wearing an Ocean Sanctuary T-shirt or pin, or attaching a bumper sticker to her car presented opportunities for talking to people about the project.

Meadow says that she raised the issue of Ocean Sanctuary at every opportunity, even when it may not have seemed like exactly the right time. She attended meetings and she

> *spent time addressing people about off-shore oil, having them write letters and distributing information, and I did this despite the fact that the topic had little direct relevance [to the meeting she was attending]—I just USED the opportunity.*[65]

Meadow is by no means the only teenager in Mendocino and Humboldt counties about whom this story might have been written. Dozens of other young men and women have come face to face with the threat of environmental degradation in their own lives and have made the commitment to fight the same kind of battle that Meadow has.

REALIZING THE POSSIBILITIES: THE MONDAY GROUP

For many teenage activists, the spark that aroused their enthusiasm for environmental causes came from a particularly interesting, challenging, exciting adult. That is the story for students who have passed through The High School Environmental Education Seminar—"the Monday Group"—in Lee County, Florida. The idea behind the Monday

Group originated in 1970 with Dr. Bill Hammond, director of environmental education for Lee County Schools.[66]

Dr. Hammond believes that environmental activism is not only for adults, but something in which high school students can also become involved. He has acted on this conviction by establishing the High School Environmental Education Seminar, an all-day class that meets once every other week to learn about and act on environmental issues in the county. Juniors and seniors from the five public and one private high school in the county are invited to take part in the seminar.

Participants in the Monday Group are expected to fulfill two major requirements: completion of an individual project and participation in a class project. Individual projects have covered a wide-ranging variety of topics, such as water quality surveys, studies of manatee life-styles, anthologies of poetry, and original albums of songs about endangered species and energy topics. The choice of an independent project determines whether the student will receive academic credit in science, social studies, English, or some other field for participation in the class.

Class projects are selected by a consensus decision of seminar members. The project must deal with an issue of concern to the local community or a problem involving leaders at the local, state, or national level. One of the most impressive class projects was a four-year campaign to purchase and begin protection of Six Mile Cypress Swamp.

Six Mile Cypress Swamp is a 2,500-acre (1,000-hectare) wetland on the eastern edge of Fort Myers, the largest city in Lee County. The swamp had been listed for many years as a potential state or federal park or protected area. But by the late 1970s, nothing had happened to make those plans a reality. Monday Group students, whose field trips had taken them to the swamp, worried that the area would soon be sold for commercial development.

As a result, the students decided that their class project would be to learn as much as possible about the swamp. They conducted a biological survey, an ownership survey, a geological survey, a hydrological survey, and a land-use survey. The information obtained in these surveys was summarized and produced as a booklet about the swamp.

The project did not come to an end with the work of the first year's class, however. The following year's seminar decided to make practical use of the booklet produced by the previous year's class. They undertook a campaign to convince county commissioners to support a referendum for the purchase of the swamp. After an initial defeat, students regrouped their forces, intensified their education program with the commissioners, and finally won their unanimous approval to put the swamp referendum on the ballot.

The task facing the third year's class was to persuade voters in the county to support the referendum. That task was not an easy one since approval meant a tax increase to pay for purchase of the swamp, and Lee County has a high percentage of retirees living on a fixed income. Also, students had only about six weeks after the opening of school in September to plan their campaign and to make their pitch to voters. The effort was a rousing success, however: the referendum passed by the largest plurality ever given a tax issue in Lee County.

The final year of the class's swamp project focused on ways of preserving the newly acquired land. As it turned out, no one in the county was prepared to administer the new swamp/park because no master plan for the park had ever been developed. The final year of the Monday Group's swamp project was spent on working on just such a plan.

The achievements of Lee County's Monday Group are impressive. Most adults would be proud to be involved in a class project like the Six Mile Cypress Swamp campaign. That Lee County students accomplished as much as they did proves age is no limitation for a committed environmental activist.

REACH FOR THE SKY: WOODLAND'S FOURTH-GRADERS

Further proof of this is the story of Mrs. Bonnie Tibbetts's fourth-grade class at Woodland (Maine) Elementary School. One does not know quite where to begin in describing the achievements of Mrs. Tibbetts's superstars of the environment. Like Bill Buck, the fourth-graders decided to have an environmental-awareness event. But they decided to make theirs last a whole week. Included during that week were such events as films, video tapes, filmstrips, and slide presentations on environmental issues; panel discussions; a balloon launch to

*Students at Woodland Elementary
School in Maine preforming their
play* The Rescuers. *Characters are
Father Time and Mother Nature.*

encourage people to conserve and recycle; a poster contest; and the presentation of two plays, *The Rescuers* and *Cinder-ella and the Prince of Pollution*.

The "Cinder-ella" of the second play gets her name because she is so busy wiping cinders off the windows of her polluted kingdom. She agrees to marry the Prince of Pollution if he promises to install scrubbers and filters in smokestacks throughout the kingdom. The fourth-graders added their own scenes 3 and 4 to conclude the commercially published play. The Environmental Awareness Week occupied every moment of spare time the fourth-graders had, even to the point that they gave up some of their recess time!

Yet Environmental Awareness Week was only one of the many environmental activities that took place in Mrs. Tibbetts's class in the 1987–88 school year. In the fall of 1987, the class decided to ask Maine governor John McKernan to proclaim Environmental Awareness Week. The governor responded that he not only thought the idea was a good one but he also wanted the fourth-graders to write the proclamation themselves.

Because Mrs. Tibbetts had always taught them to "Reach for the sky, believe in yourself, and make it happen," the fourth-graders then expanded their plans. They wrote the governors of all fifty states, enclosing a copy of their proclamation and asking the governors to issue a similar proclamation in their own states. As positive responses began to arrive from eighteen states, the class, the school, and the whole community swelled with pride.

Environmental issues are more than abstract problems for the Woodland students. After learning of the environmental problems that Styrofoam containers present, they wrote the superintendent of schools and school board to protest the practice of serving hot lunches in Styrofoam containers. In response, the board invited the students to attend one of their meetings and explain their objections to the use of Styrofoam. As a result, the board promised that it would explore alternatives to the use of Styrofoam containers for lunches in following years.

Mrs. Tibbetts weaves environmental issues into every part of the school curriculum, including science, social studies, spelling, composition, poetry, and problem-solving. It's obvious that environmentalism has also become thoroughly woven into the lives of her students.

MOVING THE CLASSROOM OUTDOORS: THE MCGINNIS MIDDLE SCHOOL

Many students take classes in environmental science today. A large fraction of those classes are held inside the school. Yet environmental education belongs in the out-of-doors, at least part of the time. The sixth-, seventh-, and eight-grade students in Mr. Chuck Clark's classes at McGinnis Middle School in Buena Vista, Colorado, certainly agree with that philosophy.

The project undertaken by the McGinnis students was the construction of a new nature area on 6 acres (2.5 hectares) of undeveloped land adjacent to the school. Financial support for the project began with a $16,200 grant from the Marquard Fund, named for E. Alfred Marquard, a St. Louis doctor who often vacationed in the area.

*Students at the McGinnis
Middle School in Colorado
participating in "Conservation Camp"*

Beginning with a plot of empty, unused land, McGinnis students worked on school days, weekends, and even holidays to create the nature area, which they named after Dr. Marquard. Working from a model provided by the National Audubon Society, they designed a network of trails that would include the three habitat zones found on the site: aquatic, riparian (river), and dry uplands zones.

They brought this plan to reality by building and paving footpaths and trails, cleaning up trash, digging irrigation ditches, constructing dams, and planting a hundred Rocky Mountain junipers and Chinese elms. The trees form a 400-foot-long (122 m) windbreak that, when mature, will protect the area from wind, provide a source of food for birds, and offer shelter and nesting spaces for many forms of wildlife.

One of the first adventures in the new nature area was a fishing class led by Colorado members of Trout Unlimited (TU), an organization dedicated to the preservation and protection of the nation's cold-water fisheries. TU members taught McGinnis seventh-graders not only how to catch fish, but also how to treat the environment in a thoughtful and compassionate way.

Next on the McGinnis students' list of projects is a series of ten learning stations designed to teach visitors about the wildlife, plants, and ecology of the area. An even more ambitious plan is to construct a mile-long (1.6 km) trail that will connect the nature area with the Arkansas River. The trail will be a self-guiding nature trail with pamphlets that describe the ecology of the area.

Students using a bird blind to
observe bird behavior at the
Marquard Nature Area in Colorado

The Marquard Nature Area is probably the most impressive, but by no means the only, product of Chuck Clark's teaching efforts. For example, eight-graders at the school have been given the responsibility of teaching environmental education classes to Buena Vista elementary school classes in grades 1 to 5.

A further example of Clark's teaching techniques was the four-day year-end "survival course" for sixth-graders at the school in 1987. Sixty-eight students camped out in Mushroom Gulch, a rocky area on U.S. Forest Service land. During the course, students had classes on wildlife preservation, forest ecology, range management, water conservation, wetlands preservation, and astronomy. The fun part of the week included campfire sing-alongs, an original skit, a treasure hunt, games, and, of course, the chance to live and learn in the out-of-doors. The experience has now become an annual event called the Conservation Camp.

THE URBAN ENVIRONMENT: THE TRAINING STUDENT ORGANIZERS PROGRAM

Environmental concerns include the destruction of deserts, the pollution of the oceans, and the erosion of crop and grazing land. They don't have much to

A newsletter on
environmental issues
published by Chuck
Clark's students

WORLD WISE

Exploring Environmental Issues Relevant To Today And The Future

Environmental Newsroom Vol. 1 No. 1 '88

Statement of Purpose

This is the first of what will be a monthly newsletter that explores the role that we have in protecting our enviornment. The articles written for this newsletter will come from students and guest writers. It will also be a newsletter that we hope will inspire action among our readers.

The world is not always a nice place to live. The long range consequences of our actions are not always fully explored. Mistakes have been made. The conflicts between development and conservation are raging and yet there are numerous success stories that we need to be aware of. We will be reading about some of the positive actions that have been taken and we will read about some of the failures.

Man and his relationship to his surroundings is at issue. Everything we do will affect something else. The problems we face in a growing world population are very complex. The survival of man depends on how capable we will become in solving these problems.

You can help. The feelings of helplessness and apathy can not become part of your vocabulary. Hard work and learning is a must. Environmental issues are relevent to today and for our future. Get involved !

MEMO

Written articles or suggestions from students for "World Wise" can be submitted for publication: Send to Mr. Clark, McGinnis Middle School, P.O. Box 0, Buena Vista CO. 81211. We will be anxious to hear from you.

The Earth is a garden,
and we are the caretakers.

Conservation Camp 1988
by, Chuck Clark

The Conservation Camp is scheduled for sixth graders. The week of May 31st thru June 3rd is promised to be a week of learning and fun. Camping in huge tents for four days and three nights, the sixth graders will learn about conservation and the ecology of Four-Mile Creek located at the base of Buffalo Peaks. We are all looking forward to these enriching experiences. Look for more details about the Camp in future publications of "World Wise."

WILDERNESS

Would you like to see a Wilderness Area near Buena Vista? There is one being proposed in the Buffalo Peaks area north of town. If you feel wilderness is important, write your Congressman.

Rep. Joel Hefley
U.S. House of
Representatives,
Washington, D.C. 20515

Rep. Ben Campbell
U.S. House of
Representatives,
Washington, D.C. 20515

do with *urban* living, right? Wrong! It is easy to think of environmental problems as related only to the wide-open spaces of the Far West. But New York City, Chicago, Los Angeles, and other major urban areas have more than their share of authentic environmental problems too. In fact, some of the most exciting work being done by teenage environmental activists today is taking place in our nation's largest city, New York.

The Training Student Organizers Program (TSO) is an activity of the Council on the Environment of New York City (CENYC), a privately funded citizens' organization that is part of the Office of the Mayor. TSO is an action-oriented environmental education program that trains students from elementary school through college to organize environmental improvement projects in their own schools and communities. In 1988, nearly a thousand students took part in TSO programs at two New York City colleges and fourteen high schools.

The range of TSO activities is impressive. Included among some recent projects are the following.

• The high level of noise from New York City subway trains was the subject of one project. Students at Lafayette, De Witt Clinton, and Kennedy high schools conducted a letter-writing and petition campaign for three years about the problem. As a result, noise abatement equipment was installed on three train lines that run near the schools. The Clinton students objected not only to the noise of the trains, but also to the graffiti, litter, and possible reduction of train service in the area. Student concerns were addressed in a meeting arranged

*A student surveys local attitudes toward
a proposed beverage-container-return bill
as part of a program sponsored by the
Council on the Environment of New York City.*

and held between Transit Authority representatives and more than one hundred students from the De Witt Clinton school.

• Cleanup and beautification campaigns have been the focus of projects at Franklin D. Roosevelt, Lafayette, and Sheepshead Bay High Schools. More than two hundred students from the three schools cleaned up three beaches in the Gateway National Recreation Area in the spring of 1987. Roosevelt students also worked on the beautification of the Prison Ship Martyrs Monument at Fort Greene Park in Brooklyn. They put up fencing and planted English ivy and forsythia to control erosion in the park. Finally, Roosevelt students wrote their congressmen, the secretary of the interior, and the commissioner of the New York State Department of Parks, Recreation, and Historic Preservation asking for their support and cooperation in maintaining the monument.

• TSO recently initiated another project in conjunction with the Office Paper Recycling Service (OPRS) of CENYC. OPRS is a program for the recycling of waste paper in New York City colleges, hospitals, corporations, office buildings, governmental agencies, churches, and banks. In 1987 TSO and OPRS worked together to install waste paper recycling programs in two New York City public elementary schools, PS 3 and PS 282. Students in the two schools are completely responsible for the operation of the recycling program. They collect waste classroom paper, store it in collection boxes in the classroom, and, when the boxes are filled, deliver them to central storage hampers. Proceeds from the sale of waste paper are returned to the schools for their use. The program is expected to

*New York City high school students
helping to clean up a wildlife refuge*

be self-perpetuating. As students pass from grade to grade, they will become organizers of new waste recycling programs in their new classrooms. As part of the activity itself, teachers include a discussion of solid waste problems in the regular classroom curriculum. By the fall of 1988, ten schools were participating in this project.

These stories show that young people from every part of the nation have started to become involved in environmental problems. Those problems exist everywhere today. But so do concerned young men and women, ready and eager to do their share in solving them.

SIX

GETTING STARTED AS AN ENVIRONMENTAL ACTIVIST

So you have decided to become an environmental activist. You have read about the hazards confronting our environment today. You have seen what other teenagers can do to make a difference on environmental issues. And you have made up your mind to go beyond simply thinking about your environment and start doing something about it. The question is, what can you do, and how do you get started?

WORKING ON YOUR OWN

Environmental activists often find that they work most effectively as the members of a group—a high school club or the local chapter of the Sierra Club, for example. But you can find many things to do by yourself, as an individual, that can make an impact on environmental issues.

Most environmental activists point out how important it is, for example, that you live your own

An interest in environmental issues can
lead to a number of rewarding careers.

life according to an environmental ethic. Do you make a special effort not to litter? Do you use bio-degradable materials that break down naturally, such as paper rather than plastic, wherever possible? Do you collect and recycle metals, glass, paper, and other materials? Activities such as these are simple, but they demonstrate to others and to yourself that you have made a personal commitment to protecting the environment.

A second thing you can do on your own is to become better informed. One environmental activist says, "Get your facts straight." One of the biggest problems she encounters in environmental work is activists who have good intentions but haven't done their homework.

You can get the background you need by reading books and articles, attending lectures and rallies, and tuning in to radio and television programs on environmental issues. You may want to sign up for classes on environmental topics at your school. A course in environmental science or biology usually offers a sound basis for becoming active. But you can also learn useful information and skills in other courses such as government, economics, political science, and journalism.

Polishing up some basic communication skills can be helpful also. Suppose, for example, that you want to correspond with your city council, your state representative, or your national senator. Or you may want to help in the writing of a pamphlet or to work on a poster. Or you may be asked to testify at a legislative hearing or to speak before a school assembly. In such cases, you will be more confident if you are able to write and speak correctly and clearly.

Another communication skill that people sometimes ignore is the ability to listen. In working on environmental issues, it is important not only to let people know what *your* views are, but also to make sure that you understand what others have to say. You can learn a lot by listening to others who *support* your cause. But you may be able to learn even more by hearing what your opponents have to say. Besides, only by understanding what their arguments are can you know how best to respond to their views.

When the time comes that you are actually prepared to speak out on an issue, you will probably have many opportunities. The very fact that you are a student means that you have many built-in chances to express your views on issues. Teachers will ask you to give reports, write themes, prepare individual and group projects, organize class discussions, construct bulletin board displays, and offer your views to the class in other ways. If you are like other students, you may have had trouble in the past choosing a topic. With an interest in environmental issues, that decision should never be a problem again.

Out-of-class activities are available too. Maybe a club you belong to wants suggestions for a special program. Or the principal may be looking for ideas for a school assembly. Or you may have chances to meet with students from other schools in interscholastic conferences. On such occasions, you may be able to refer to environmental issues in which you are interested. You may have to stretch a point sometimes, bringing up your topic even when it's not intended as the main theme of a conference or a meeting. But, as Meadow Makovkin pointed out, you can usually find a way to make mention of your pet project, no matter what the meeting or conference is really about.

Letter writing is another form of activism that each person can do in the privacy of her or his home. It is a technique that can have a powerful impact on legislators and others in decision-making positions. Legislators often comment on the influence a single letter can make. They point out that on even the most critical issues they have to consider, very few citizens take the time to write and express a viewpoint. In such cases, a few dozen personal letters may represent a "landslide" of opinion on that topic.

WORKING IN A GROUP

People who are interested in environmental issues often begin working by themselves, but most then go on to a second level and look for others with whom they can work. They either join or form groups of like-minded environmentalists.

Where can you find an environmental group to join? Often that is no problem at all. You can simply pick up the Yellow Pages of your telephone directory and look under "Environmental organizations." A call to one or more of the groups listed there will start you on your way. You will either be greeted with a delighted "Come on down! We need your help" or you will be told to "Try the X Club or call Mrs. Y. They have just what you are looking for."

If the Yellow Pages cannot help, you can look elsewhere. The appendix lists addresses and telephone numbers for some major national groups interested in the environment. These groups can tell you where in your own area you can get in touch with groups that need members and volunteers. If you strike out there, you can also ask the biology teacher in your school, your town's environmental protection officer, or someone at a nearby college. On rare occasions you may find, as Bill Buck did, that no environmental organization exists in your area. In that case, you may want to organize your own group, a process we talk about in the next chapter.

Suppose you have found an environmental group in your area with which you would like to work. What kind of opportunities can you expect to find with that group? The answer to that question depends somewhat on the organization you have chosen. However, the possibilities for a first-time volunteer tend to be somewhat similar to most groups. The first day you walk through the front door of an environmental group, you should expect to be asked to do one or more of the following:

- Lick envelopes and stamps for the group's next mailing
- Make telephone calls to residents of the town
- Walk the streets collecting signatures on a petition
- Do door-to-door canvassing to get people out to vote, to deliver publicity, to solicit donations, or to provide information
- Stand on a street corner handing out brochures
- Go for coffee and doughnuts for people working in the office, to pick up supplies needed in the office, or on other errands (volunteers are usually in great demand as "go-fers")

- Help make signs for marches and rallies
- Write letters
- All of the above, and much more

One thing you should NOT expect is to become chairperson, executive secretary, or publicity director on the first day you arrive. As with almost any other kind of organization, very few people start at the top of an environmental group. That is even more likely to be the case with teenagers, whom organizations may consider only valuable as envelope-lickers or go-fers.

Some teenage activists have expressed their frustrations at being treated as second-class citizens, not quite as capable or reliable as adult volunteers and members. Some well-known national environmental organizations, in fact, have the reputation for being distinctly not interested in working with teenage volunteers. In most cases, however, hard-working teenagers can quickly overcome any initial doubts on the part of adults and move to more responsible jobs in an environmental organization.

Volunteering to work with an organization can be an invaluable experience for a teenager. For one thing, the experience gives you the opportunity to try out a variety of jobs. Maybe you will be assigned to the phone bank and find that you hate talking with people on the telephone for hours at a time. No problem. You can ask to be assigned to another task: door-to-door soliciting, filing, or fund-raising, for example. Before long, you will be able to find out the kind of environmental work that suits your skills and personality best.

Volunteering is also valuable because of the free training you are likely to get. Many organizations are willing to teach first-timers some of the fundamental skills that are needed in any volunteer organization. After spending a few months in such an organization, you will have learned enough to move up within the organization or on to other environmental groups with the opportunity of taking on more responsible jobs.

ATTITUDES COUNT

Environmental activism means getting things done. That, in turn, means having the knowledge and skills to bring about change. But success in dealing with environmental issues often involves attitudes also. Environmental activists often stress how important it is to develop and maintain certain attitudes about the work they do.

Maintain a Positive Outlook

Environmentalists are often criticized for having a negative view of the world, for being *against* dams, *against* pesticides, *against* offshore drilling, *against* any form of development. Yet, the real meaning of environmentalism is having a positive view of the world, being *for* natural rivers, *for* safe foods, *for* scenic views, *for* the unity of nature.

When you become an environmental activist, look for and promote the positive view of issues. Suppose you oppose offshore drilling, for example. By all means you should work to prevent offshore drilling. But also find ways to take a positive stance on this issue. For example, become active in energy conservation programs, or work to promote the development of alternative energy sources.

Bill Hammond cites this attitude as an essential rule of the Monday Group. He says

We will accept only positive viewpoints in this class. If you are against something, if you don't like something, or if you don't want something to happen, then you must turn it around. You must be for something, you must want something to happen, you must have a wish.[67]

Be Humane and Open-Minded

Extend your positive outlook to the people with and against whom you work. As difficult as it sometimes becomes, activists must always remember that the members of the opposition have a right to hold and express views different from the ones held by environmentalists. You may not agree with others' views, but you have an obligation to try to understand how they have arisen. Open-mindedness is a valuable attitude because it sometimes happens that your own views are too simplistic, impossible to achieve, incomplete, or even wrong.

Once you have crossed the threshold to open-mindedness, it then becomes possible to look at environmental issues not just as "us against them," but as complex problems on which people of goodwill differ, work, and perhaps come to some compromise solution.

Develop Perspective

Environmentalists—especially teenage activists—also need a sense of perspective. Many of us would like the world to get "fixed up" now, or at least no later than two weeks from Wednesday. But change comes slowly.

Accepting that fact is critical. It means that you can be satisfied with short-term gains. You may not be able to eliminate all noise pollution in your com-

*Youth Conservation Corps participants
at work. Contact government agencies
for information on such programs.*

munity this week, for example. But you may be able to win small battles that will take you in that direction.

Persevere

Acknowledging the slow pace of environmental change means that you should also adopt a philosophy of perseverance. Small defeats and small victories must be seen only as steps backward or forward in a longer journey that may take many years.

Teenage environmentalists speak passionately about this attitude. They often began their work in the environmental movement with a fervor and idealism that is characteristic of adolescence and soon felt almost equally great amazement and disillusionment that their sincere hard work did not change the world overnight. They adjusted to that reality, developed a perspective on the problems facing them, committed themselves to persevering and now encourage other teenagers to do the same.

Have Fun!

The work of an environmentalist can seem depressing. You hear about protestors chaining themselves to redwood trees, frustrated citizens lying down in front of bulldozers, and angry people screaming at public officials. Yet most environmentalists believe quite the opposite to be the case. When asked what advice they have for beginning environmental activists, veterans often say, "Have a good time," "Enjoy yourself," and "Maintain your sense of humor."

The whole point of the environmental movement is to find joy and fulfillment in the natural world. It becomes a disaster when someone works so hard on the offshore oil drilling campaign that she can find no time to go sailing, or concentrates so hard on the speeches and films for next week's Environmental Awareness Program that he finds no way to bring fun and laughter to the event.

Trust Yourself

Teenagers face a special problem when they become involved in environmental issues. Too often in our society adolescents are regarded as frivolous, incompetent, and irresponsible. Adults make these accusations so often that teenagers themselves sometimes believe them. They worry that they may not be good enough to take on serious environmental issues like those discussed in this book.

Without exception, the teenagers and adults interviewed for this book reported having these feelings at one time or another. Each person talked of being shy and afraid that he or she would have nothing to offer an environmental group, that adults would look down on or sneer at them. But they also warned other teenagers like you *not* to let these attitudes hold you back.

Bill Buck's advice is "Don't be afraid." He reports that the adults with whom he works now respect him as an equal partner in their efforts. They do so because they know what he has achieved. He has earned their respect, and he has no fears about working with men and women many years older than he.

Know Your Limitations

Each person does some things well and other things not so well. Teenagers should know their limitations. If you have a short temper, for example, then

A Student Conservation Association volunteer (see Appendix) provides information to hikers.

sitting at an information booth where you meet people with viewpoints different from your own might not be the right assignment for you.

Your "limitations" might be nothing other than "being human." That means you should not volunteer for every organization and every activity in the county. The problem is that once word gets out that you are available, you may be invited to join, contribute to, volunteer for, and attend every event in the state for the next year. If you try to please everyone, you will probably end up doing many things poorly and nothing well. Taking on too much with too little personal return often results in "burnout"—the loss of energy and desire to work any longer in the environmental movement.

SEVEN

FORMING YOUR OWN
ENVIRONMENTAL ORGANIZATION

Teenage activists often decide to form their own environmental organizations. They may choose to do so for a number of reasons. For one thing, they may simply not want to work their way through the power structure in an existing adult group. Teenagers often also want, legitimately, to have experiences as group leaders, not just as followers. They may choose not to deal with the negative attitudes adults sometimes have about teenagers.

Finally, the schools which teenagers attend often make it possible for young people of similar interests to organize and work together. They provide student organizations with such resources as meeting space, duplicating machines, and reference books.

Of course, schools expect the organizations they sponsor to follow certain rules and regulations. Because of these requirements, some teenagers prefer to create environmental organizations outside of the school structure, giving them freedom to do the things they want.

Wherever they are organized, within school or outside it, teenage environmental groups usually face many of the same problems. Understanding what those problems are in advance will help your organization run more smoothly. Even if you do not start your own organization, knowing about these problems is likely to help you see how *any* environmental organization operates.

GETTING YOUR GROUP ORGANIZED

The first step in organizing an environmental group is of course to find other teenagers with interests similar to your own. You may already have the beginnings of a group in your circle of friends. After all, friends often have shared interests. You can also advertise for group members in the school or local newspaper, by posting signs, or by word of mouth. An important thought to keep in mind is that a successful beginning depends more on having a few really committed members than on having a large number who really do not care very much.

The earliest stages of your organizing process can be critical. You want to start off with a bang, a burst of enthusiasm that will excite new members. Often, an organizational meeting will provide this spark. Publicity about this initial meeting is likely to attract newcomers who share your interests.

Most environmental groups try to resolve some basic questions at their first few meetings, questions such as: What will our name be? What officers do we need? How will decisions be made? How much money do we need to operate, and how shall we collect that money?

Choosing a Name

Your organization's name is important because it is usually the first thing the public knows about you. Select a name that is short, that tells what you are working on, and that is catchy and/or memorable.

Officers and Decision-Making

Many organizations decide to elect one or more officers: a president, vice-president, secretary, and treasurer, for example. Other groups simply work together as a team, with no one person "in charge" of things, but with each individual assigned specific tasks. Some organizations want an experienced adult to advise the group. Others prefer to have strictly a youth organization.

You will also need to decide how decisions will be made in the group. One way to make decisions is by consensus. Consensus means that everyone has to agree on an action or a decision. The advantage of consensus decision-making is that everyone is in agreement on decisions. The disadvantage is that reaching consensus can be a long and difficult process. Making decisions by majority vote is much faster, but in the process some people (the minority) are likely to be dissatisfied with the final action.

Money Matters

Some environmental groups get along very well with very little money. They make their own signs, borrow duplicating equipment, solicit donations of materials and supplies, and generally get along on a shoestring. Most groups, however, need at least some income. These groups should develop a budget that shows where their money will come from and how it will be spent. A budget helps the club to keep its priorities straight. It shows whether the group is devoting its efforts to the environmental problems that it was organized to work on or whether it is being distracted by fund-raising, social, or other events.

Organizations have many ways of making money: by having cake sales, by charging dues, and by asking for donations from individuals, organizations, and businesses, for example. One caution you may want to consider, however, is to avoid overtaxing your members. Your group will be better off with a hundred hardworking members who pay $1 a month dues than it will be with twenty-five richer but less ambitious members who pay $10 a month.

LOOKING FOR ALLIES

Some organizations work effectively in complete isolation, having no contact with other adult or teenage environmental groups or other groups of any kind. But most environmental groups work best in association with others who share their interests and concerns. You would almost certainly want to get in touch with your local Sierra Club, Wilderness Society, Earth First!, Friends of the Earth, or other national or state environmental group.

You may discover that worthwhile connections can also be made with nonenvironmental groups such as peace groups, feminist groups, racial equality groups, gay and lesbian groups, and other organizations working on a variety of social issues. Many teenage activists report that their own interests are not confined to environmental issues alone, but extend to many other progressive movements as well. Networking—the process of making and maintaining connections with other like-minded individuals and groups—is thus a normal and critical activity for most activists.

SELECTING GOALS

As some point, every environmental organization has to ask itself why it exists. What goals does the organization have? What environmental changes does it hope to bring about?

Two warnings should be kept in mind in setting goals. First, be concrete. Deciding that your organization "wants to do something to clean up the environment," for example, is too vague. What is the "something" you want to do, and what part of "the environment" do you want to work on?

Second, be realistic. Set goals that you can reasonably expect to reach. Maybe your group would like to have all supermarkets in the state stop using plastic shopping bags next week. But that is probably hoping to accomplish too much in too short a time. Better to try reducing the use of plastic shopping bags by one or more stores in a selected area.

Your organization may want to adopt both long-term and short-term goals. Long-term goals give the organization a vision as to what it might want to achieve at some time in the future, perhaps one to five years down the road. Long-term goals may be too ambitious to accomplish in the near future, but they help to remind an organization why it was formed and what its real purposes are.

Short-term goals are important too. They allow your group to target specific parts of a larger problem that can be solved in a reasonably short time. Achieving a short-term goal can also provide the kind of positive emotional experience that all environmental activists need from time to time.

PLANNING FOR ACTION

When people join an environmental group, they probably think first of ACTION. They want to get into the streets, the halls of Congress, the mayor's office . . . anyplace they can start making a change. That *is* of course what environmental activism is all about. But it does not make much sense simply to paint your "NO MORE POLLUTION" poster and start marching down Main Street. Instead, you need to think about what you want to do and then plan actions that are likely to achieve your objectives.

The Opposition
You almost certainly disagree with the people whom you are working against, private industries or property developers, for example. But you must understand their position on the issue you are battling about. You cannot debate an opponent if you do not know what the motivation is for their actions, what they hope to achieve, how they expect to accomplish their objectives, where their support comes from, and so on.

Your Options
Environmentalists are often accused of being too negative, people who say "Stop" or "Don't," but don't have any ideas of their own. Perhaps you are working against the installation of a toxic-waste dump outside your town. Think about what *should*

be done with the toxic wastes. If you do not have an alternative suggestion of your own, people may not see any choice *but* to follow your opponent's plan.

Taking the Initiative

You can be a more effective activist if you or your organization sets the agenda. If you let the opposition decide how the issue will be phrased and where the debates will be held, you may have lost half the battle. Challenge your opponents to attend a press conference, get a sympathetic legislator to introduce a bill representing your position on the issue, present your case to the media and the public.

Who Makes the Decisions?

You are likely to feel quite foolish if you picket the mayor's home to express your opposition to a new highway around town, and then find out the mayor has no voice in that decision. Whatever plan of action you finally decide to take has to be aimed at those who will decide the issue. Learning the power structure and finding out who is really in charge are critical steps in planning for your actions.

Who Is With You?

Knowing what kind of community support you have is important. You may find that most people agree with your position. Then your job is to mobilize that support. Or you may find that most people disagree with you or don't care about the issue. In that case, your job is to educate people and convince them of your position.

These comments apply especially to people with influence in the community. For example, lawyers and legislators can be critical allies if you become involved in court cases or in passing new legislation.

Matching Jobs and People

The shyest, most quiet volunteer in your organization probably should not be asked to argue your side in a public television debate with the public relations director of the local power company. A man who can type 120 words per minute should not be assigned to making posters. Good planning for action involves identifying the special skills each member of the organization has and making the best use of those skills.

Maintaining Enthusiasm

Working on environmental causes can be discouraging. Many battles are lost, and volunteers may be tempted to ask, "What's the use?" When battles are won, they demand many hours of unpaid hard work. A good environmental organization will remember both the "highs" and "lows" that volunteers experience. It will work to help members maintain enthusiasm and high spirits.

Having coffee and doughnuts available for volunteers does not cost much, and it tells workers that their efforts are appreciated. Victory parties and victory-next-time parties keep people going after both triumphs and defeats.

The one enduring fact about environmental battles is that, no matter how today's particular issue was resolved, another skirmish lies just around the corner. Winner or loser, you have to be prepared to begin all over again tomorrow on the same or another problem.

Action!

The purpose of environmental activism is to bring about some kind of change. That change may involve any one of the three branches of government: administrative, legislative, or judicial. To illustrate each, you and your organization may either decide to

1. Persuade the Department of the Interior not to allow oil drilling in the wilds of Alaska (an administration action),
2. Persuade your state legislature to pass a law regulating the runoff of pesticides from farm land (a legislative action),
3. Persuade a local court that a factory in your town has violated the Clean Air Act and must be ordered to use air pollution devices on its smokestacks (a judicial action).

Certain procedures have to be followed when acting in each of these three areas. In addition, activists often try to influence and take advantage of public opinion relating to environmental issues.

HEARINGS

The crucial event that occurs for many environmental issues is a hearing. A hearing is just what the word implies: an opportunity for all sides contesting an issue to make their views known before a group that is to decide on that issue. For example, committees of the national and state legislatures and county and city councils usually hold hearings on legislation they are considering. Before voting on a bill to allow strip mining in your county, for example, a committee of state legislators will probably hold a hearing at which the mining company, environmental groups, and other interested organizations and individuals may appear, make statements, and present evidence.

Hearings may be held by legislative groups, whose job it is to make laws; by administrative groups, whose job it is to carry out legislation; and by regulatory groups, whose job it is to see that laws are not being violated. Preparing for and taking part in a hearing can be a rather complicated event. In order to make use of the hearing process, an environmental group should understand completely what the ground rules for the hearing are, how it can appear at the hearing, and what it can and cannot do there.

Environmental groups have published some useful pamphlets and booklets explaining how best to make use of the hearing process. Among these is the section on "Handling Hearings" in *The Grass Roots Primer* and the chapter on "Organizing Support for a Wilderness Proposal" in *Action for Wilderness* (see For Further Reading).[68]

NEW LAWS

In some cases, the best way to deal with an environmental issue is to get a law passed. In one California city, for example, environmental activists were able to convince their city council that one way to fight the city's solid-waste problems was to prohibit the use of plastic containers by fast-food establishments in the city. Of course, getting action on a local level is likely to be easier than trying to get a bill passed at the state or national level. In either case, environmentalists must have a good working relationship with one or more legislators who will introduce and work for legislation favored by environmentalists.

Sometimes legislators are not responsive to environmental concerns, so getting a bill passed by the usual process can be difficult. In such cases and in some states, another avenue is available: the referendum or initiative procedure. Both of these procedures allow individual citizens or groups to place questions on the ballot. The process usually requires that petitions be submitted containing a certain minimum number of names of eligible voters. Then the question is placed on the ballot at the next regular election. Voters in many cities and states have offered laws on smoking regulations in public places, for example, by means of the initiative process.

COURT ACTION

The final step available to environmentalists is often a lawsuit. A group of environmentalists concerned about offshore oil drilling first tried to persuade the Department of the Interior not to allow that drilling at an administrative hearing. When that attempt failed, they tried in vain to get legislation passed to prevent the drilling. As a last resort, the environmentalists went to court, arguing that offshore oil drilling violated certain federal and state water-pollution laws. Court action is a step that teenage environmental groups seldom take on their own because it is expensive and requires expert legal advice.

PUBLIC OPINION

In some sense, the most important work that environmentalists can do is to influence public opinion. Legal arguments, new laws, and regulatory hearings have only limited value if the general public does not understand the environmental issues it faces and the choices it has on those issues. Most environmentalists are therefore firmly committed to (1) educating the general public, explaining how the United States has damaged its environment, (2) persuading people that changes have to be made in the way we view and treat our environment, and (3) showing people what they can do to alter the way we use our natural resources.

To accomplish these ends, environmentalists have developed a wide variety of public relations tools, including press conferences and press releases; letter writing directed at legislators and newspapers; get-out-the-vote campaigns; petition drives; paid advertisements; newsletters, brochures, handbills, posters, flyers; marches and protest meetings; door-to-door solicitations and presentations; nature walks and clean-up campaigns; appearances on radio and television shows and interviews for newspaper articles; speeches before community groups; and guerilla theater and street performances. The aim of all these tech-

What will be the legacy we leave to the future inhabitants of "spaceship Earth"?

niques is to develop an informed and sympathetic public so that legislative and court victories for environmentalism will truly reflect the will of the people.

One of the most basic goals of environmental activism is to educate the general public. This does not mean telling people all the right answers to the world's problems. Environmentalists are wrong as often as other humans are. But environmentalists can point out options. They can search for ways of maintaining a desirable quality of life without destroying the environment. They can provide an image of human life as part of the natural world, not as separate from and superior to it.

In the process of cleaning up toxic dumps, reducing air pollution, or preventing the destruction of wetlands, environmental activists can also provide people with a renewed and noble image of their place in nature. What more challenging and fulfilling goal could a young person choose for his or her life today?

A PARTIAL DIRECTORY OF
ENVIRONMENTAL ORGANIZATIONS

For an annually published list of state and federal agencies with environmental responsibilities, see *The Environment Index* (New York: EIC/Intelligence, Inc.).

The Acid Rain Foundation, Inc.
1410 Varsity Dr.
Raleigh, NC 27606
919-787-8387
Goals: To improve public understanding of problems involving acid rain. The Foundation supports research and provides educational materials and information on acid rain.

Center for Marine Conservation
1725 De Sales Street, N.W.
Washington, DC 20036
202-429-5609
Goals: To protect marine wildlife and their habitats.

Citizens Clearinghouse for Hazardous Wastes
P.O. Box 926
Arlington, VA 22216
703-276-7070
Goals: To work with citizens' groups at local levels to fight toxic polluters and to promote safe alternatives to unsafe waste disposal practices.

The Conservation Foundation
1250 24th Street, N.W.
Washington, DC 20037
202-293-4800
Goals: To bring together experts from many different fields in order to study all aspects of environmental problems. The Foundation then makes recommendations and communicates those recommendations to those in decision-making positions in government, industry, business, academia, and the general public.

The Cousteau Society
425 E. 52nd Street
New York, NY 10022
212-826-2940
Goals: To promote research and provide information on preservation of the world's oceans.

Defenders of Wildlife
1244 19th Street, N.W.
Washington, DC 20036
202-659-9510
Goals: To preserve and protect all forms of wildlife. The organization is engaged in education, research, and lobbying.

Environmental Action Foundation
1525 New Hampshire Avenue
Washington, DC 20036
202-745-4870
Goals: To promote grassroots activism as the key to solving environmental problems. The group lobbies and organizes on pollution, safe energy, recycling, and energy conservation.

Environmental Defense Fund
257 Park Avenue South
New York, NY 10010
212-505-2100
Goals: To develop and promote creative solutions to environmental problems through a combination of scientific and legal means.

Environmental Policy Institute
218 D Street, S.E.
Washington, DC 20003
202-547-5330

Goals: To provide research, education, and lobbying on a wide variety of environmental issues.

Environmental Protection Agency
401 M Street, S.W.
Washington, DC 20024
202-382-2090
Goals: To implement federal laws to protect the environment.

Friends of the Earth
530 Seventh St., S.E.
Washington, DC 20009
202-543-4312
Goals: To educate, lobby, and provide legal action on a variety of environmental issues. A related group, the League of Conservation Voters, raises funds for congressional candidates who support its goals.

Greenpeace, USA
1436 U Street, N.W.
Washington, DC 20009
202-462-1177
Goals: To organize, lobby, and take direct action on environmental issues such as toxic wastes, nuclear energy, and hunting of whales and seals.

Izaak Walton League
1401 Wilson Blvd, Level B
Arlington, VA 22209
703-528-1818
Goals: To educate the public about threats to our natural resources and to promote citizen involvement in local environmental protection efforts. The League also represents the interests of those interested in outdoor sports before Congress.

National Audubon Society
950 Third Avenue
New York, NY 10022
212-832-3200
Goals: To support scientific research, provide education, and promote environmental activism in order to attain a better environment. The Society publishes Action Alerts that notify members of issues requiring special, urgent attention.

National Coalition against Misuse of Pesticides
530 7th Street, S.E.
Washington, DC 20003
202-543-5450
Goals: To make the public aware of the potential hazards associated with pesticide use and to promote alternative pest management techniques that require few or no toxic chemicals. The Coalition also advocates public policies that will better protect the public from pesticide exposure.

National Institute for Urban Wildlife
10921 Trotting Ridge Way
Columbia, MD 21044
301-596-3311
Goals: To carry out research on the relationship between humans and wildlife in urban and developing areas. The Institute also publishes information about maintaining and improving wildlife populations in urban areas and, in general, improving the general quality of urban life.

National Parks and Conservation Association
1015 31st Street, N.W.
Washington, DC 20007
202-944-8530
Goals: To create and defend national parklands and other areas of natural and cultural importance. The Association also educates the public about the importance of these areas and about ways that the areas can be enjoyed. Its primary goal is to see that the national parks are preserved for future generations.

National Wildlife Federation
1400 16th Street, N.W.
Washington, DC 20036-2266
703-790-4000
Goals: To educate and inform the general public and legislative bodies about important environmental issues. The Federation publishes magazines and books for children and adults, produces materials for educators, and operates camps for children and teenagers. It also testifies before various legislative bodies.

The Nature Conservancy
1800 North Kent Street, Suite 800
Arlington, VA 22209
703-841-5300

Goals: To find, protect, and maintain the best examples of communities, ecosystems, and endangered species in the world. As of 1988, the Conservancy was responsible for 968 preserves in 50 states, the largest private sanctuary system in the world.

Rachel Carson Council
8940 Jones Mill Road
Chevy Chase, MD 20815
301-652-1877
Goals: To promote knowledge about and interest in the environment; to encourage enlightened conservation methods; and to serve as a clearinghouse of information for scientists and nonscientists. The Council's main emphasis at this point is on the use of chemical pesticides and their effect on the environment.

Sierra Club
730 Polk Street
San Francisco, CA 94109
415-776-2211
Goals: To educate the general public about environmental issues and to lobby legislative groups on such problems.

Soil and Water Conservation Society
7515 NE Ankeny Road
Ankeny, IA 50021
515-289-2331
Goals: To conserve land, water, and related resources to meet the needs of present and future generations. The Society promotes meetings and research that lead to recommendations and land and water management policy.

Student Conservation Association
Box 550
Charlestown, NH 03603
603-826-5741
Goals: To provide high school and college students, as well as other persons who are out of school, with an opportunity to volunteer their services working in the nation's parks, on its public lands, and with its natural resources.

Trout Unlimited
501 Church Street, S.E.
Vienna, VA 22180
703-281-1100

Goals: To preserve and improve coldwater fisheries. The organization works both at the local level and at the national level to achieve this objective.

The Wilderness Society
1400 Eye Street, N.W.
Washington, DC 20005
202-842-3400
Goals: To create and protect wilderness areas, national parks and recreation areas, and other public areas. The Society was founded by Aldo Leopold and continues to promote his philosophy that land is not a commodity to be used carelessly, but a resource to be cherished and preserved for future generations.

The Wildlife Society
5410 Grosvenor Lane
Bethesda, MD 20814
301-897-9770
Goals: To develop and promote sound stewardship of wildlife resources and the environment; to help prevent damage to the environment by humans; to increase awareness of the value of wildlife; and to promote high standards among professionals who work with wildlife and the environment.

World Wildlife Fund
1250 24th Street, N.W.
Washington, DC 20037
202-293-4800
Goals: To carry out research and other projects that will help protect endangered wildlife and wildlands throughout the world. Since its founding in 1961, the Fund has been involved in 1370 projects in 103 countries. The fund also educates the general public, trains wildlife professionals, promotes the skills individual nations need to conserve their own resources, attempts to influence public opinion, and monitors international trade of endangered plants and animals.

NOTES

1. Charles E. Kupchella and Margaret C. Hyland, *Environmental Science: Living within the System of Nature* (Boston: Allyn and Bacon, 1986), 536.
2. Lynn White, "The Historical Roots of Our Ecologic Crisis," *Science,* March 10, 1967, 1203–1207. The White essay has been reprinted in a number of anthologies as, for example, in David Spring and Eileen Spring, *Ecology and Religion in History* (New York: Harper & Row, 1974).
3. Genesis 1:28; also see Psalms 8:6–8.
4. White, in Spring and Spring, 28.
5. Ron Wolf, "God, James Watt, and the Public's Land," *Audubon,* May 1981, 65.
6. Joseph M. Petulla, *American Environmental History* (San Francisco: Boyd & Fraser, 1977), 64, 102–103.
7. Stewart H. Holbrook, *Holy Old Mackinaw.* Macmillan, 1956. As quoted in Petulla, 221–222.
8. Petulla, 47.
9. Ibid., 94.
10. Ibid., 103.
11. Ibid., 176–177.
12. Ibid., 47.
13. Ibid., 253, 291, 297.
14. Kupchella and Hyland, 281.

15. Jonathan Turk and Amos Turk, *Environmental Science,* 3d. ed. (Philadelphia: Saunders, 1984), 205.
16. *Information Please Almanac, 1988* (Boston: Houghton, Mifflin), 143.
17. Petulla, 221.
18. Ibid., 221.
19. Ibid.
20. Richard H. Wagner, *Environment and Man,* 3d ed. (New York: W. W. Norton & Company 1978), 420; also see C. Gill, F. Booker, and T. Soper, *The Wreck of the Torrey Canyon* (London: David & Charles Ltd., 1967), and R. W. Holmes, "The Santa Barbara Oil Spill," in D. P. Hoult, ed., *Oil on the Sea* (New York: Plenum Press, 1969).
21. Kupchella and Hyland, 369.
22. Wagner, 419.
23. Turk and Turk, 435.
24. Joseph M. Moran, Michael D. Morgan, and James H. Wiersman, *Introduction to Environmental Science,* 2d ed. (New York: W. H. Freeman, 1986), 229–230.
25. Richard Wilson and William J. Jones, *Energy, Ecology and the Environment* (New York: Academic Press, 1974), 297.
26. Wagner, 419.
27. Turk and Turk, 435.
28. Kenneth E. Maxwell, Greayer Mansfield-Jones, and Dorothy Mansfield-Jones, *Environment of Life,* 4th ed. (Monterrey, Calif.: Brooks/Cole 1985), 325.
29. J. Raloff, "Congress Kills the U.S. Synfuels Corp.," *Science News,* January 11, 1986, 22.
30. Kupchella and Hyland, 422.
31. Ibid., 414.
32. Moran et al., 498.
33. Biological Sciences Curriculum Study, *Investigating the Environment: Land Use* (Dubuque, Iowa: Kendall/Hunt, 1984), 26–27.
34. Kupchella and Hyland, 524.
35. Ibid.
36. Peter Wild, *Pioneer Conservationists of Western America.* (Missoula, Montana: Mountain Press, 1979), 4.
37. Henry David Thoreau, "Walking," in *Excursions* (New York: Corinth Books, 1962), 161.
38. Bradford Torrey and Francis H. Allen, eds., *The Journal of Henry D. Thoreau,* 14 vols. (Boston: Houghton Mifflin, 1949), vol. 14, 306–307.

39. Roderick Nash, *The American Environment: Readings in the History of Conservation*, 2d ed. (Reading, Mass. Addison-Wesley, 1976), 13.
40. Petulla, 221
41. Eldon D. Enger, J. Richard Kormelink, Bradley F. Smith, and Rodney J. Smith, *Environmental Science: The Study of Relationships* (Dubuque, Iowa: Wm. C. Brown, 1986), 490.
42. Wild, 34.
43. Ibid., 42.
44. Douglas H. Strong, "The Sierra Club—A History; Part 1: Origins & Outings," Sierra Club Reprint from *Sierra*, October 1977.
45. Wild, 49.
46. Petulla, 283.
47. Geoffrey Norman, "The Flight of Rachel Carson," *Esquire*, December 1983, 472–479.
48. Wild, 154.
49. Ibid., 157.
50. For example, see Elizabeth R. Gillette, ed., *Action for Wilderness* (San Francisco: Sierra Club, 1972).
51. Robert A. Jones, "Fratricide in the Sierra Club," *The Nation*, May 5, 1969, 569.
52. 1987–1988 National Conservation Campaigns, Sierra Club Fact Sheet.
53. Nash, 46.
54. *Sierra Club* v. *Morton*, 405 U.S. 727 (1972).
55. *Statistical Abstract of the United States, 1988*, 311.
56. Wild, 175.
57. "Conservation's Future," *The New Republic*, January 4, 1969, 12–13.
58. Stewart Udall, *The Quiet Crisis* (New York: Holt, Rinehart & Winston, 1963), 175.
59. Ibid., 191.
60. Michael J. Weiss, "Lois Gibbs, the Love Canal Heroine, Is Making Hazardous Wastes an Industry of Her Own," *People*, February 22, 1982, 42.
61. Kenneth E. Maxwell, Greayer Mansfield-Jones, and Dorothy Mansfield-Jones, *Environment of Life*, 4th ed. (Monterey, Calif.: Brooks/Cole, 1985), 245–247.
62. Jane Kay, "Wave of Unrest Grows on Shore," *San Francisco Examiner*, April 3, 1988, A-14.
63. Ibid.
64. Ibid.

65. *Personal Communication,* June 20, 1988.
66. Information about the Monday Group is from *Project WILD, Secondary Activity Guide* (Boulder, Colo.: Western Regional Environmental Education Council, 1985).
67. Bill Hammond, in *Project WILD, Secondary Activity Guide,* 279.
68. James Robertson and John Lewallen, *The Grass Roots Primer* (San Francisco: Sierra Club Books, 1975), and Gillette, 65–89.

FOR FURTHER READING

Textbooks you may find useful:

Enger, Eldon D., J. Richard Kormelink, Bradley F. Smith, and Rodney J. Smith. *Environmental Science: The Study of Relationships.* Dubuque, Iowa: Wm. C. Brown, 1986.

Kupchella, Charles E., and Margaret C. Hyland. *Environmental Science: Living within the System of Nature.* Boston: Allyn and Bacon, 1986.

Maxwell, Kenneth E., Greayer Mansfield-Jones, and Dorothy Mansfield-Jones. *Environment of Life,* 4th ed. Monterey, Calif.: Brooks/Cole, 1985.

Moran, Joseph M., Michael D. Morgan, and James H. Wiersma. *Introduction to Environmental Science,* 2d ed. New York: W. H. Freeman, 1986.

Purdom, P. Walton, and Stanley H. Anderson. *Environmental Science: Managing the Environment.* Columbus, Ohio: Charles E. Merrill, 1980.

Turk, Jonathan, and Amos Turk. *Environmental Science,* 3d ed. Philadelphia: Saunders, 1984.

Wagner, Richard H. *Environment and Man,* 3d ed. New York: W. W. Norton & Company, 1978.

Other books that can be read for useful information or enjoyment:

Allen, Robert. *How to Save the World.* Totowa, N.J.: Barnes & Noble Books, 1980. An examination of the world's environmental problems with recommendations for solving those problems.

Bregman, J. I., and Sergei Lenormand. *The Pollution Paradox.* New York: Books, Inc., 1966. A good historical and contemporary review of pollution problems.

Bunyard, Peter, and Fern Morgan-Grenville. *The Green Alternative: Guide to Good Living.* London: Methuen, 1987. A description of "Green" philosophy, a way of thinking based on "concern for life on earth." Also see Jonathan Porritt, below.

Cahn, Robert, ed. *An Environmental Agenda for the Future.* Washington: Island Press, 1985. A series of essays by leaders of the Sierra Club, National Audubon Society, Wilderness Society, Friends of the Earth, and other environmental organizations as to what we should be doing in the future.

Dasmann, Raymond F. *The Conservation Alternative.* New York: John Wiley & Sons, 1975. An overview of the current ecological crisis, "rules of the game" in working on the environment, and some conservation alternatives to current ways of doing things.

El-Hinnawi, Essam, and Manzur H. Hashmi. *The State of the Environment.* London: Butterworths, 1987. A scholarly and thorough analysis of the international state of the planet's environment.

Gillette, Elizabeth R., ed. *Action for Wilderness.* San Francisco: Sierra Club, 1972. An example of the "Battlebooks" published by the Sierra Club in the 1960s and early 1970s.

Goldsmith, Edward; Robert Allen; Michael Allaby; John Davoll; and Sam Lawrence. *Blueprint for Survival.* Boston: Houghton Mifflin, 1972. Valuable, if somewhat dated, background information with some good suggestions for environmental action.

Havlick, Spenser, W. *The Urban Organism: The City's Natural Resources from an Environmental Perspective.* New York: Macmillan Company, 1974. An interesting text dealing with the special problems of urban areas.

Krier, James E., and Edmund Ursin. *Pollution and Policy.* Berkeley: University of California Press, 1977. A fascinating account of air pollution problems created by automobiles in California and the rest of the U.S. between 1940 and 1975.

Melosi, Martin V. *Pollution and Reform in American Cities, 1870–1930.* Austin: University of Texas Press, 1980. An account of the relationship between environmental problems and politics.

Nash, Roderick. *The American Environment: Readings in the History of Conservation,* 2d ed. Reading, Mass: Addison-Wesley, 1976. A collection of original documents by nearly all of the important environmental activists in American history.

Petulla, Joseph M. *American Environmental History.* San Francisco: Boyd & Fraser, 1977. A superb reference on American attitudes and practices relating to the environment since Colonial days.

Porritt, Jonathan. *Seeing Green: The Politics of Ecology Explained.* Oxford, England: Basil Blackwell, 1984. An explanation of Green politics in Europe and the United States.

Robertson, James, and John Lewallen. *The Grass Roots Primer.* San Francisco: Sierra Club Books, 1975. An outstanding "practical book for people whose world is threatened and who want to do something effective to prevent the piecemeal destruction of Earth's natural environment."

Schaeffer, Francis A. *Pollution and the Death of Man: The Christian View of Ecology.* Wheaton, Ill.: Tyndale House, 1970. One of many responses from those who disagreed with Lynn White's analysis.

State of the Environment: A View toward the Nineties. Washington: The Conservation Foundation, 1987. A comprehensive analysis of the current status of the nation's environment and the outlook for the future. A valuable resource.

Wild, Peter. *Pioneer Conservationists of Western America.* Missoula, Mont.: Mountain Press, 1979. A good sourcebook for concise and useful biographies of fifteen important environmental activists.

INDEX

Watt, James, 26–27
Week on the Concord and Merri-
mack Rivers, A (Thoreau),
64, 66
Wetland, 59–61
White, Lynn, 26
Wild and Scenic Rivers System, 87

Wilderness Society, 75
Wildlife, 44
Wind turbines, 55
Woodland Elementary School,
97–100

Youth Conservation Corps,
120

ABOUT
THE AUTHOR

David E. Newton is a free-lance writer specializing
in science and technology subjects. He holds a B.A.
from the University of Michigan in chemistry,
which he has taught at the high school and college
levels. Mr. Newton has published over 30 educational books. He has also written *Science Ethics, The
U.S. and Soviet Space Programs,* and *Particle Acceler-
ators* for Franklin Watts.